WELCOME

I n 1926, a princess was born in Mayfair, London. Named Elizabeth after her mother, she was third in line to the throne, but expected to be pushed further down the line of succession when her uncle had his own children. She would have no such luck.

Queen Elizabeth II ascended the throne in 1952 after the death of her adored father. Her uncle had abdicated almost 20 years beforehand, disgraced and childless. Regardless, she would rise to the occassion, celebrating jubilee after jubilee and managing the expectations of her and her family.

In this touching tribute to one of Britain's most beloved monarchs, we explore the woman who has ruled over generations of her subjects. From her worst year - or 'annus horribilis' - to her triumphs and joy, we remember a queen who devoted herself to her country and the people within it.

A TRIBUTE TO
QUEEN
ELIZABETH II

FOX CHAPEL
PUBLISHING
www.FoxChapelPublishing.com

CONTENTS

EARLY YEARS

THE WINDSOR FAMILY

From 'us four' to the Queen's own four, uncover a royal family tree

The Queen Mother with Edward, David and Sarah

ELIZABETH II

1926-2022
♛ **1952-2022**

In 1952, Elizabeth became queen after her father's death. Her coronation was held on 2 June 1953 at Westminster Abbey.

PRINCE PHILIP

1921-2021

Having married in 1947, Philip sacrificed his titles, his career, and later even his surname for his wife and queen, Elizabeth.

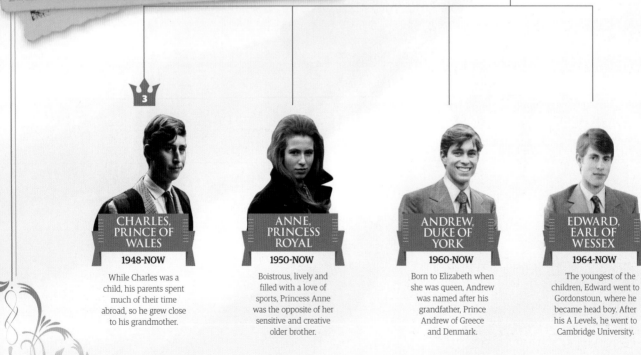

CHARLES, PRINCE OF WALES

1948-NOW

While Charles was a child, his parents spent much of their time abroad, so he grew close to his grandmother.

ANNE, PRINCESS ROYAL

1950-NOW

Boistrous, lively and filled with a love of sports, Princess Anne was the opposite of her sensitive and creative older brother.

ANDREW, DUKE OF YORK

1960-NOW

Born to Elizabeth when she was queen, Andrew was named after his grandfather, Prince Andrew of Greece and Denmark.

EDWARD, EARL OF WESSEX

1964-NOW

The youngest of the children, Edward went to Gordonstoun, where he became head boy. After his A Levels, he went to Cambridge University.

Order of succession
x

Marriage

Divorced

GEORGE VI
1895-1952
♛ 1936-1952

ELIZABETH BOWES-LYON
1900-2002

The Queen pictured with her family at Windsor on her 39th birthday.

PRINCESS MARGARET
1930-2002

After her first love married someone else, Margaret married photographer Antony Armstrong-Jones in 1960.

ANTONY ARMSTRONG-JONES
1930-2017

Upon marrying Princess Margaret, Antony was given the title earl of Snowdon. They divorced in 1978.

Charles and Anne picnic with their grand-uncle and aunt, Louis and Edwina Mountbatten

DAVID ARMSTRONG-JONES
1961-NOW

Now known by his professional name, David Lindey, he is the former chairman of Christie's and makes furniture.

LADY SARAH ARMSTRONG-JONES
1964-NOW

An award-winning artist, Sarah excelled at art in her youth and is now the vice president of the Royal Ballet.

©Getty

Bertie and Elizabeth on their wedding day

BERTIE IN LOVE

Lady Elizabeth Bowes-Lyon would prove a fine example of that old saying, "hard to get", after refusing the hand of the future king of England not just once, but twice

Adored by the British public and a leading light in the gloom of World War II, Elizabeth Bowes-Lyon was once described by Adolf Hitler as "the most dangerous woman in Europe". For many, it's hard to think of the late Queen Mother - in her feathered hats and floral dresses - as anything other than a harmless grandmama. But there was a side to Elizabeth that few, besides those closest to her, knew about. Beneath the innocent and smiling exterior was a woman of ambition and cunning, determined to secure the hand of none other than the king of England himself. She would eventually be successful in her endeavour - but not in a way she could have imagined.

Elizabeth Angela Marguerite entered the world on 4 August 1900, the ninth of ten children born to Claude Bowes-Lyon, Lord Glamis, and his wife Cecilia... or at least, that is the official published story. Edward, the Duke of Windsor - known during his brief time on the throne as Edward VIII - famously referred to the Queen Mother as 'Cookie', alluding to the rumour that Elizabeth was in fact the daughter of Claude and Cecilia's French chef, Marguerite Rodiere.

It is certainly true that there has been much confusion surrounding where she was born - even, it seems, from the Queen Mother herself. In 1921, she wrote on her passport application that she had been born in London, but in 1937 she unveiled a plaque that marked her birthplace as St Paul's Walden, Hertfordshire. Then, in July 1980, in the lead-up to her 80th birthday,

Clarence House issued a statement reasserting that Her Majesty had been born in London.

It may be that her birth was an early form of surrogacy, which, although unusual, was not unheard of. It's possible that Lady Glamis had been advised not to have any more children after she suffered a nervous breakdown, following the death of her eldest child, Violet, in 1893. The truth behind Elizabeth's birth could never be exposed, however, as it wouldn't be until the 21st century that adoptive children of the aristocracy were given the same right as natural children to inherit their parents' titles. By acknowledging Elizabeth as her legitimate issue, Cecilia ensured her daughter could assume the rank, style and title that all of her legitimate children were due.

Regardless of their genetic link (or lack thereof), Elizabeth and Cecilia were devoted to one another. Lady Glamis was renowned for being a wonderful hostess, and even as a child Elizabeth shared her talent for entertaining, often being encouraged to socialise with the older guests at her parents' parties. Replying to an application for the role of Elizabeth's governess, Cecilia wrote: "[She] is really a delightful companion - very old for her age - and very sensible. So that you will not have a child with you always."

One of her tutors, Dorothy Birtwhistle, remembered her as being bright and charming, able to get away with all types of mischief thanks to her angelic exterior: "I was not surprised with the life she ended up having. I could see, even when she was 12, that she would make her mark on the world if given a chance."

It was during World War I that Elizabeth really had her chance to shine. Following the declaration of war, Claude took the decision to move his family to Glamis Castle in Scotland - his family's ancestral seat. While her four elder brothers departed for the Western Front, Elizabeth, her sister Rose and their mother set about knitting socks and mufflers for the local battalion.

It was then decided that the castle would be used as a convalescent home for wounded soldiers returning from the Front. The furniture was removed from the dining room and replaced with rows of beds. While Rose undertook nurse training, Elizabeth, being only 14, was instead given the job of making the injured young men feel at home. She ran errands for them, replenished their stocks of chocolate and cigarettes, wrote their letters home when they could not, read to them and kept them company. Her charm and mischievous streak proved a winning formula among the soldiers. One soldier wrote: "For her years she was very womanly, kind-hearted and sympathetic", and another that the houseguests "worshipped" Elizabeth.

The war continued far longer than was expected, and grief struck the family with news of the death of Fergus, Elizabeth's older brother, at the Battle of Loos in September 1915. But for all of its tragedy, Elizabeth still found benefits in the war - namely the many handsome men in uniform. She and her governesses would spend many hours at the window of the family home in London watching the soldiers' to-ing and fro-ing, or chatting to "beautiful sailors" on the night train back to Scotland. One of the few sailors who Elizabeth did not acknowledge as beautiful was Prince Albert - the second son of King George V and Queen Mary. She was present at a party he attended in 1916, and her friend Helen Hardinge would later say that Elizabeth found him "almost repellent".

Within a few weeks of this meeting, the sailor prince would get his first taste of action as a turret officer aboard HMS Collingwood in the Battle of Jutland. Prior to that, he had been posted to the Admiralty with a desk job, having been discharged from naval service following a bout of appendicitis in 1914. When he was finally permitted to return to sea, he spent much of his time on Collingwood confined to the sick bay with acute depression, surfacing only for the battle. Following a diagnosis of duodenal ulcers, the decision was made in February 1918 to keep him on dry land.

That same month, Elizabeth had her coming of age dance. The party was a huge success and well attended, and she was now on her way to becoming one of the most popular girls in society. Within a month, she had a beau - Charles, Lord Settrington, heir to the Goodwood estate and the dukedom of Richmond and Gordon. If she could manage to secure him, she would also secure one of the greatest titles - and homes - in England. The Hon Stephen Tennant, one of her contemporaries, wrote that she "picked her men with the skill of a chess player, snobbish, poised" and "schooled her intentions like a detective, totting up her chances". Indeed, her eye would soon wander when in

"WITH CHARLIE DEAD AND THE PRINCE OF WALES REJECTING HER ADVANCES, SHE NEEDED TO WIDEN HER POOL OF POTENTIALS"

March 1918, she was introduced to Edward - the Prince of Wales and heir to the British throne.

Before the war, the likelihood of a first-in-line marrying someone of Elizabeth's rank was slim to none. For the past two centuries, the German royal houses had provided wives for English princes, but with the two countries at war, that was no longer an option. The Act of Settlement of 1701 also forbade marriages between royal heirs and Roman Catholics, so that ruled out the Belgians and Italians, and of course many of the other European states were now republics. With the pool dramatically reduced, the prime minister advised George V that his sons be allowed to marry the daughters of British aristocrats instead.

News of this spread like wildfire through society, and Elizabeth adjusted her sights accordingly. Like Elizabeth, the 24-year-old Edward was fun-loving and sociable, and he danced with her twice at their first meeting. But Elizabeth's old-fashioned sweetness was not to his taste - he liked his girls sleek and modern. As she turned up the charm, he made sure to keep her at arm's length.

The end of the war eventually came, and Elizabeth continued to be friendly with Charles Settrington. But in 1919, he volunteered for military

service in Russia, where civil war raged between the Reds and the Whites. In August, Elizabeth received the devastating news that he had been killed. The young woman was inconsolable, writing to her friend Beryl: "He is my only real friend and one feels one can never have another like him." With Charles dead and the Prince of Wales rejecting her advances, she needed to widen her pool of potentials, and she became an infamous flirt. Within a month of Charles's death, she had ensnared one of her brother Mike's friends - James Stuart, the 17th earl of Moray. In October that year, he was appointed Prince Bertie's equerry, and it was while Elizabeth and James were dancing together at a Royal Air Force Ball in July 1920 that she caught Bertie's eye.

Until relatively recently, Bertie had been in love with another woman. He had met Sheila Chisholm, the Australian wife of the 5th earl of Rosslyn, through his elder brother, and she was regarded as exciting and exotic. When his father caught wind of the affair with a married woman, he bribed him into ending it by offering him the dukedom of York - and Bertie accepted. Though he was still pining for Sheila, it did not prevent him from asking Elizabeth to dance.

As a child, Elizabeth was academically bright and charming, but also mischievous

According to the duke of Windsor (second from left), Elizabeth was initially more interested in him than his brother Bertie (second from right)

When Elizabeth entered society at the age of 17, she quickly became one of its most popular debutantes

THE ROYAL WEDDING

How the spectacular wedding of Bertie and Elizabeth won over the nation

The date was set for 26 April 1923, at Westminster Abbey. The guests included the prime minister, Bonar Law, politician Winston Churchill, and Cecilia's cousin Sir Oswald Mosley - future leader of the British Union of Fascists - while tens of thousands of people lined the route to the abbey, braving the heavy rain showers.

Elizabeth was attended by eight bridesmaids, and she wore a dress of ivory chiffon moire designed by Madame Handley-Seymour, dressmaker to Queen Mary. A strip of Brussels lace, inserted in the dress, had been worn by one of her ancestors at a grand ball for Bonnie Prince Charlie, a Stuart claimant to the throne. Her bouquet, which she famously laid upon the Tomb of the Unknown Soldier, was of white roses. Bertie, meanwhile, wore his RAF uniform - he had joined upon its creation in April 1918, and qualified as a pilot in July the following year.

Despite their turbulent courtship, *The Times* reported that Bertie had "shining eyes and a look of happiness", and he and Elizabeth "seemed to think of no one but each other". After a wedding breakfast at Buckingham Palace, the pair boarded a train from Waterloo to Polesden Lacey, a Georgian mansion in Surrey, where they would spend their honeymoon.

Elizabeth and Bertie were finally wed at Westminster Abbey on 26 April 1923, despite two refused proposals

The day after, Elizabeth wrote to Beryl saying "he is quite a nice youth" - despite Bertie being four years her senior - and made no mention of his appearance, as she had done with every other eligible bachelor. Over the following months, Bertie visited her several times, but Elizabeth's affections remained with James. So when James made his lack of interest clear, it was time for her to try a new tack, spurring on Bertie in an attempt to make James jealous.

Her plan backfired. In February 1921, Bertie informed his parents that he was going to propose to Elizabeth. Upon hearing that she was a nice, old-fashioned girl, they readily agreed. But when he asked for Elizabeth's hand over lunch a few days later, his proposal was rejected. If she couldn't have James, she would settle for no less than the immediate heir to the throne - or at least, that is how the duke of Windsor would later explain it. Others argue that it was her fear of the

Elizabeth makes her way to Westminster Abbey on her wedding day

Elizabeth was considered classically pretty, as this portrait of her in her mid 20s shows

Glamis Castle in Angus, Scotland, the ancestral seat of the earls of Strathmore and Kinghorne where Elizabeth spent much of her childhood

Elizabeth with her father Claude, Earl of Strathmore and Kinghorne, and mother Cecilia

"THE PRESS WERE SOON KNOCKING ON ELIZABETH'S DOOR, AND THE FUTURE DUCHESS DID SOMETHING UNPRECEDENTED"

restrictions of royal life that led her to turn him down. In a letter to Bertie the next day, she said: "I must write one line to say how dreadfully sorry I am about yesterday. It makes me miserable to think of it - you have been so very nice about it all - please do forgive me." Cecilia, too, wrote to Bertie, saying "how truly grieved we are that this little romance has come to an end" and that "I do hope the queen is not very much annoyed".

But the George and Mary were still hopeful that Bertie and Elizabeth would marry, and in September 1921, Mary arranged to meet Elizabeth in person. She became convinced that she was "the one girl who could make Bertie happy". In an effort to seduce her into the royal way of life, she encouraged her daughter, Princess Mary, to ask Elizabeth to be one of her bridesmaids. Exactly a week after the wedding, Bertie proposed again, but once more was rejected. This time, Elizabeth wrote: "I do hope we can go on being friends, as it would be too sad if a happening like this should

come between our friendship, and I don't see why it should, do you?"

The pair continued to correspond and dance together at balls and functions, and it soon became obvious - to everyone other than poor Bertie - that Elizabeth was stringing him along. By keeping him close, she was keeping her options open, buying herself time to see whether a better offer (from either James or perhaps the Prince of Wales) would come along. Her flirting with him was so overt that other female hopefuls felt unable to make a move of their own. When Queen Mary heard of this, she was furious, and wrote to her friend Mabell asking that Elizabeth's invitation to the next ball be withdrawn.

This revelation would have been extremely unnerving for Elizabeth and her mother. The queen could ostracise anyone from society. Realising that the game was over, Elizabeth knew that her only option was to get Bertie to propose to her once more - and this time she had to accept.

Elizabeth and Bertie's daughter, the future Queen Elizabeth II, was born in 1926

But amazingly, when Bertie did propose again - for the third time - on 2 January 1923, Elizabeth did not give an immediate response. "It is so angelic of you to allow me plenty of time to think it over - I really do need it, as it takes so long to ponder these things, and this is so very important for us both. If in the end I come to the conclusion that it will be alright, well and good, but Prince Bertie, if I feel that I can't (and I will not marry you unless I am quite certain, for your own sake) then I shall go away and try not to see you again."

By this point, King George and Queen Mary were at their wits' end, with Mary writing to Mabell: "I confess now we hope nothing will come of it as we both feel ruffled at E's behaviour." Mabell would inevitably have delivered this information to Cecelia, who would in turn have told her daughter that it was now or never.

Bertie did everything he could to appease his mother, asking her permission to go to Elizabeth once more and get a "definite answer one way or another". He arrived at St Paul's Walden at 10.30am

on Saturday 13 January, and it wasn't until 11.30pm the next day that he finally got the answer he had been waiting over two years for.

When the engagement was announced, the press were soon knocking on Elizabeth's door, and the future duchess did something unprecedented - she invited them in for interview. The royal family were horrified, but it was this move that would do more for their popularity than anything else had in years. She was painted as a "charming picture of English girlhood" - sweet-natured and a real human being, unlike the other, more aloof members of the family.

The royal family learned an important lesson that day - that accessibility is what would keep them on the throne. When, on her wedding day on 26 April 1923, Elizabeth laid her bouquet at the Tomb of the Unknown Soldier - starting a tradition that continues to this day - the loyalty of the public was sealed. Little did she know that 13 years later, her ambitions would finally be realised, and Elizabeth would be crowned queen of England.

The duke and duchess of York, photographed in 1928

BIRTH OF A QUEEN

The birth of a new royal was a cause for celebration, even if she was not expected to become queen

Words **Scott Reeves**

A small crowd gathered to cheer King George V and Queen Mary as they arrived by car at the Mayfair townhouse belonging to the earl and countess of Strathmore and Kinghorne on 21 April 1926. The mid-afternoon royal visit was brief - just 30 minutes - but the monarch left expressing his "great pleasure". Behind the door, away from the interested gaze of the onlookers, was the newest member of the royal family, little more than 12 hours old. It was certainly a happy moment in the history of the Windsor family, although the king had no idea that his new granddaughter would one day become Britain's longest-reigning monarch.

The new baby was not the first grandchild of the king - his only daughter, Princess Mary, had already given birth to two boys, George in 1923 and Gerald in 1924 - but the newest member of the royal family immediately leapfrogged them in the order of succession. Whereas George and Gerald previously sat sixth and seventh in the line for the throne, behind their mother and her four surviving older brothers, the new girl slipped in at number three by virtue of being the child of the king's second son, Prince Albert, Duke of York.

However, the chances of her remaining there seemed remote. If the duke of York had a son, he would take precedence over his older sister in the line of succession, and it was still assumed that carefree bachelor Edward, Prince of Wales, would settle down and marry. Nevertheless, the beginning of the popular duke of York's young family was a welcome distraction from the domestic strife that dominated the previous weeks' newspapers.

The duke of York had married Lady Elizabeth Bowes-Lyon on 26 April 1923, meaning their daughter missed sharing her birthday with their wedding anniversary by only five days. Although nominally a commoner due to her lack of royal blood, the new duchess hailed from one of Scotland's most ancient families as the youngest daughter of the earl of Strathmore and Kinghorne. A little over two years after the wedding, Elizabeth fell pregnant in July 1925 amid a flurry of royal duties, obligations added to by the Prince of Wales'

The banquet that followed Elizabeth's christening included an immaculate cake

absence on a tour of South Africa and Rhodesia. The duke and duchess had a summer itinerary that included a tour of the Black Country, hosting their first official party for 600 guests at St James' Palace and attending engagements at the Royal Caledonian School and the British Empire Exhibition at Wembley Stadium.

Elizabeth became aware of her pregnancy just in time for two well-deserved breaks; first at Goodwood as a guest of the earl of March, then at Glamis Castle with her family. She was placed under the care

"IF THE DUKE OF YORK HAD A SON, HE WOULD TAKE PRECEDENCE OVER HIS SISTER IN THE LINE OF SUCCESSION"

The young princess had no shortage of godparents, including the king and queen

of Sir Henry Simson, one of the most renowned medical practitioners of his day. He had attended the birth of Princess Mary's two sons and would be a founder member of the Royal College of Obstetricians and Gynaecologists in 1929. Yet Simson could do nothing to stop the duchess suffering the same malady as most would-be mothers. She wrote of her morning sickness, "I am feeling much better now, tho' the sight of wine simply turns me up! Isn't it extraordinary." Elizabeth, who was always fond of a tipple, would soon recover her bibulous ways.

News of the pregnancy was kept secret and the duke and duchess resumed a programme of public engagements in the autumn, visiting Hackney and Cheltenham, attending the funeral of Queen Alexandra (the widow of Edward VII) and joining the royal Christmas celebrations in Norfolk. The Yorks moved to central London in November 1925, renting Curzon House in Mayfair. Although the public reason was that it was more convenient than their usual abode at White Lodge in Richmond Park for the usual winter engagements, it also meant that Elizabeth had her doctors close at hand.

The impending birth of a royal baby was finally reported in the press in January 1926, by which point it was impossible to ignore the fact that the duchess was sporting a bump. As the estimated due date neared, the imminent royal birth became a predominantly Bowes-Lyon affair. In early April, the Yorks moved out of Curzon House and spent Easter weekend at St Paul's Walden Bury, the Hertfordshire country house belonging to Elizabeth's family, before moving into her family's London residence at 17 Bruton Street to prepare for the birth.

The duchess of York fell pregnant during a busy summer of royal engagements, including this visit to the West Midlands

On hand was a trusted midwife, Annie Beevers, who had helped bring Elizabeth's sister's children into the world. Elizabeth was confident in the abilities of the woman who she described as "tall, dark and very Yorkshire" and asked her to recommend a tonic for the latter stages of pregnancy "as I get rather tired (and irritable I fear!)". Also with her was Clara Cooper Knight, a veteran nanny who had looked after the Bowes-Lyon children, including the young Elizabeth. It was Alah, as she was affectionately known, who would be charged with the day-to-day care of the new baby.

At 2.40 in the morning on 21 April 1926, the newest royal finally made an appearance. Courtiers woke the king and queen to deliver the news just before 4 o'clock, around the same time that the government passed on details to the Press Association so it could be included in late-morning editions of the newspapers.

Later that day, a bulletin declared that mother and child were making "very satisfactory progress" and that "previous to the confinement a consultation took place, at which Sir George Blacker [a notable obstetrician] was present, and a certain line of treatment was successfully adopted". The

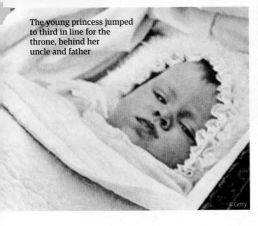

The duke and duchess of York were a popular couple - their first child arrived three years after their marriage

The young princess jumped to third in line for the throne, behind her uncle and father

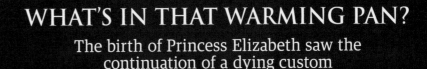

WHAT'S IN THAT WARMING PAN?

The birth of Princess Elizabeth saw the continuation of a dying custom

While Princess Elizabeth was born in the early hours, William Joyston-Hicks sat patiently (and presumably sleepily) in a neighbouring room. It was his responsibility as home secretary to ensure that there was no funny business going on in the birthing room, a tradition that stemmed from the divisive days of 1688.

When a healthy boy was born to King James II, many feared that the young prince would be brought up a Catholic. Hoping to avoid Britain returning to the pope's sphere of influence, conspiracy theories abounded in which it was suggested that the new prince was actually smuggled into the queen's bedchamber in a warming pan because the true heir was stillborn. The tension caused by the royal birth and its resulting rumours ended in James's overthrow in the Glorious Revolution.

This archaic tradition was in its final years when the future queen was born in Bruton Street. The home secretary was summoned for a final time in 1936 for the birth of Princess Alexandra to the duke and duchess of Kent; King George VI scrapped the requirement shortly before the birth of Prince Charles in 1948. Overworked home secretaries and royal mothers presumably breathed a sigh of relief.

The birth of Prince James gave rise to an odd tradition that lasted 250 years

"certain line of treatment" probably referred to the induction of labour. The birth eventually ended in a caesarean section after a long labour, although both the royal family and press steered away from the exact details of the birth.

Bertie delighted in the "tremendous joy" that his first child brought and hoped that his mother and father "are as delighted as we are, to have a grand-daughter, or would you have sooner had another grandson". He needn't have worried. The king was a besotted grandfather and the queen replied that the princess was "a little darling".

The duke of York may have been enthralled by his daughter, but he probably missed her first outing, when she was wheeled into the Bruton Street garden after ten days inside. Instead, he was observing heated debates in the House of Commons in the hope of averting a national emergency. Months of industrial strife had led to negotiations between the Miners' Federation of Great Britain and mine owners collapsing, and a strike began on 1 May that escalated into a general strike on 4 May. An estimated 2 million employees refused to work in support of the miners, but the royal household did its bit to help the government's contingency plans. Equerries and lords-in-waiting were sworn in as special constables, while several members of noble families volunteered as mounted police. After nine days, the Trades Union Congress agreed to end the general strike, though the miners held out for much longer. The government had proven it could hold out for longer than its workers, but the workers had demonstrated the depth of their feeling and solidarity.

The government hoped that the new princess would bring the country together again. Newspapers eagerly speculated what her name would be, desperate to find a lighter, more positive story. The choice, when it was finally announced, was a traditional collection of royal names, Elizabeth Alexandra Mary, after her mother, great-grandmother and paternal grandmother.

Princess Elizabeth's christening took place in the private chapel at Buckingham Palace on 29 May; Cosmo Lang, the archbishop of York, was on hand to conduct the service. The one-month-old princess wore the long, dark-cream silk gown that had been used in royal christenings since that of Victoria, Princess Royal in 1841. Plenty of room had to be left around the font for the seven godparents: the king and queen, Princess Mary, the duke of Connaught, the earl and countess of Strathmore and Lady Elphinstone. Their young godchild was not particularly impressed with the ceremony, however, and cried throughout, the only time, future commentators noted, that Elizabeth made a fuss in public.

After the ceremony, well-wishers outside Buckingham Palace were granted a view of the baby as she was lifted high in her car, but for the rest of the summer glimpses of the new princess were scarce. The duchess of York was determined that her daughter would grow up out of the limelight as much as possible, and Elizabeth's time in the spotlight appeared to be over.

It was expected that the young princess would grow up a privileged but increasingly marginal royal as the line of succession was populated with more heirs who outranked her. Yet fate had a far more prominent role for her to play.

"PRINCESS ELIZABETH'S CHRISTENING TOOK PLACE IN THE PRIVATE CHAPEL AT BUCKINGHAM PALACE ON 29 MAY"

THE HAPPY HOME

The duke and duchess of York loved their life at their cosy London base and it became a refuge as the House of Windsor headed into choppy waters

Nothing remains of the house where a happy family life became the making of two monarchs. From 1927 to 1936, the future George VI and Queen Elizabeth, then duke and duchess of York, lived with their family at 145 Piccadilly. It was bombed in the war and has since been demolished and built on. But it was in this house that Bertie, as his family called him, and his beloved Elizabeth raised their two daughters - Princess Margaret Rose and the future Queen Elizabeth II. It was here that the bonds were built that led George VI to famously describe his royal family as 'Us Four'. And it was here that both he and his eldest daughter found the support and confidence that helped them become the backbone of the House of Windsor.

This family home was a much longed-for retreat for the duke and duchess of York, but they had to wait until several years after their marriage before finding their dream home. Immediately after their 1923 wedding, the couple had been loaned White Lodge in Richmond Park, but they found it too big and too isolated for their needs. Soon after the birth of their first daughter, Princess Elizabeth, in 1926, they planned to move to central London. With the help of a bank loan, they took on 145 Piccadilly and moved in the following year.

The duke and duchess had been keen to live in the heart of the capital again, although neither Bertie nor Elizabeth had any intention of

frequenting the daring party sets then beloved of Bertie's brothers, Edward and George. Their new home, close to Hyde Park Corner, gave them views of Wellington Arch and a vista across Green Park to Buckingham Palace. In his later years, the duke's father, King George V, took to waving at Princess Elizabeth every morning, with his granddaughter happily joining in the fun. For although this was a royal residence, it was first and foremost a family home.

That's not to say it wasn't grand. Described as a terraced town house, 145 Piccadilly was far from ordinary. Its stone façade included a pillared entrance topped with a small balcony where the family appeared to greet crowds on more than one occasion. Accommodation spread from a semi-basement kitchen to the suite of rooms at the top of the house that was used by the young princesses. It was there that they had their day nursery, night nursery and a little bathroom, as well as a landing where the young Elizabeth, already an equestrian in the making, used to line up her rocking horses every night to change their saddles and harnesses.

The house needed a lot of work when the Yorks took it on in 1927. They also found themselves in want of furniture. Queen Mary let them keep many of the pieces they had used at White Lodge and lent them some chandeliers that had been hanging at Osborne House on the Isle of Wight. She also handed over a cheque for home

improvements while the young couple hunted out several items at sales. The duchess of York even had to find new curtains when she discovered those she had used at White Lodge were too small for the windows of her new home.

However, as they prepared to move house, the duke and duchess of York were also getting ready to embark on a tour of Australia and New Zealand, and so many of the changes to their new house happened while they were away. When they returned six months later, George V was the first to point out the hard work that Queen Mary had put into 145 Piccadilly.

Inside, it had all the airs of the old world that was now fading into history. Heavy furniture filled the rooms - even the baby's nursery held an old-fashioned glass-fronted display case where some of Elizabeth's many toys were put on show. But for Bertie and Elizabeth it was the home they had craved and their little girl was at its heart. Their tour had been a huge success, but the couple had missed their baby daughter greatly. Now, even though they were fast becoming the hardest-working members of the royal family, Elizabeth once again became their main focus. Her mother excitedly described her as "quite delicious" on more than one occasion, while her father could barely contain his pride in her.

However, like all royal couples of the time, Bertie and Elizabeth had help with their children.

They had employed a nanny, Mrs Knight, soon after the birth of their first daughter, and she had a big role in young Elizabeth's life. She took charge of feeding and dressing the princess as well her daily routine, dictating everything from playtime to bath time. She found herself with quite a chatterbox on her hands as the little princess soon showed how keen she was to talk. It was within the walls of 145 Piccadilly that she started to say her own name but, unable to pronounce it, came up with 'Lillibet' instead - a name still used by her closest family. And if there was a quiet moment, it was filled by Jimmie, the parrot that Bertie had adopted during the tour of Australia, who liked to ask people if they wanted a drink.

The Yorks soon developed a routine that saw them spend the first part of the year at their London home before heading to Scotland for the summer. It was there, at Glamis Castle on 21 August 1930, that the couple welcomed their second daughter. Princess Margaret Rose first

came to 145 Piccadilly that autumn with Mrs Knight taking care of her while her under nurse, Margaret MacDonald, was given greater charge of Princess Elizabeth. The two had already formed a deep bond, with the little princess calling her 'Bobo'. The link that started at 145 Piccadilly would last for decades to come.

During her tour of New Zealand, the duchess of York had noted how children there "come first in everything" and as her young family grew, it was a policy she herself adopted. Although the girls had their rooms at the top of the house, they were allowed to go pretty much where they pleased. In the morning, they ran down to their parents to breakfast together, while lunch was also shared with mama and papa if both were at home. At bath time, their parents trekked up the stairs to their daughters to play while pillow fights were a regular family pastime.

The duchess of York had also had a transformative effect on her husband's family,

Bertie and Lillibet play with their pets in the gardens of 145 Piccadilly in July 1936, just months before they would have to leave their idyllic family home

"BERTIE AND ELIZABETH WERE DETERMINED THAT FUN SHOULD BE AS BIG A PART OF THE YOUNG PRINCESSES' LIVES"

The royal family with their dogs in the grounds of the Royal Lodge, Windsor in June 1936, just months before Bertie became king

Princess Elizabeth poses in front of the The Little House (Y Bwthn Bach), which was gifted to her by the people of Wales

PLAYDATES WITH A PRINCESS

Princess Elizabeth's early friends were mostly royal relations but her home at 145 Piccadilly allowed her to extend her social circle

Some of the earliest images of the Queen as she grew up were taken in the gardens at 145 Piccadilly. In these photographs, the then Princess Elizabeth is seen playing happily, cuddling her pet corgis and running carefree in this safe and secluded part of central London. But the garden, shared with several other properties in the row, was also where she could enjoy playdates and where she would make friendships that would last for years.

In 1930, Lillibet asked a little girl in the gardens if she would play with her. Sonia Graham-Hodgson later recalled that they spent an afternoon playing 'French cricket' before heading inside with the future monarch shouting, "See you tomorrow!" It was the beginning of a friendship that saw the two girls spend nearly every day together when they were both in London.

Sonia, who was eight months older than the princess, remembered sharing games like hopscotch with her royal friend who she described as thoughtful and well behaved. Their lives changed when Princess Elizabeth moved to Buckingham Palace after her father became king in 1936 with their playdates becoming less frequent. They would always stay in touch, however, until Sonia's death in 2012.

Princess Elizabeth with her friend, Sonia. They sometimes left the grounds of 145 Piccadilly to play in Hyde Park

which had previously been inclined to bouts of stuffiness. Elizabeth managed to befriend them all and so 145 Piccadilly became a hub for uncles, cousins and grandparents who wanted to spend time with the young princesses. King George V and Queen Mary were utterly smitten with both of their granddaughters while Elizabeth's parents, the earl and countess of Strathmore, were also regular visitors. They, like others who paid a call, might find teddy bears or dolls raining down on their heads as they arrived in the entrance hall. As the princesses grew up, they took to hurling soft toys down the stairwell from their top floor nursery as soon as anyone entered the grand hallway.

But young Lillibet was fast approaching the age when schooling had to play a part in her carefree existence and at Easter 1933, Marion Crawford

The family were great dog-lovers, and the family kept labradors as well as corgis

joined the household as governess to the young princess. Crawfie, as she came to be known by her charges, had previously worked for the duchess of York's family and had impressed both Elizabeth and Bertie with her straightforward manner and love of the outdoors. She made them wait two weeks before agreeing to a trial and after that month-long test, she began a life with them that would last for over 15 years.

Crawfie had wanted to be a child psychologist and soon had Princess Elizabeth reading newspapers. She devised a timetable that covered six days with morning lessons starting at 9.15am and ending at 12.30pm for lunch. However, she found the duchess of York to be rather relaxed about the formal education of her daughters. The duchess had taught young Lillibet to read and spent time telling Bible stories to both her children when they came into her bedroom in the morning, but Crawfie would end up feeling both girls could have learned more. Queen Mary agreed with her. She wanted more religion and history included in her granddaughters' lessons, but Bertie and Elizabeth were determined that fun should be as big a part of the young princesses' lives.

Even as the girls grew up, lessons at 145 Piccadilly - always taken in the boudoir belonging to their mother - were kept to mornings, however hard Marion Crawford tried to alter the routine. Afternoons were dedicated to dancing, singing and fresh air. It was easy for Crawfie to get the girls out and about - their London home had a large, communal garden at the back where they

could walk, run and play. It also gave the young princesses a rare chance to meet other children their own age.

Crawfie would later anger her employers by writing about her experiences with the family, but it is from her that we get a clear picture of the relationship not only between parents and children but between the duke and duchess of York themselves during their time at 145 Piccadilly. Marion Crawford described the pair as "most happy in their own married life". While

Crawfie smiles with Princesses Elizabeth and Margaret in a miniature car

The ordinary London townhouse became a focal point for photographers desperate to catch a glimpse of the popular royal couple and their baby daughter

the romances of the Prince of Wales were thrilling gossip columnists, the Yorks had a public image as hard working, steady and quiet. But Crawfie said that they were "very much in love" and the couple liked to take evening meals by themselves in the dining room of their London home, time just for them in a house dominated by the daughters they so clearly adored.

The family also had use of other homes. As well as spending time at the royal retreats of Balmoral and Sandringham, they had a second home at Royal Lodge in Windsor Great Park, which George V allowed them to use from 1931 onwards. But it was to 145 Piccadilly that they always returned. It was here that they developed the habit of playing card games together, often settling down for rounds of Rummy, Snap or the rather appropriate Happy Families.

The London home of the duke and duchess of York had always been an office as well as a home but as the 1930s got under way, it became more central to their royal work. The couple were taking on more responsibilities as George V's health faltered and Edward, Prince of Wales, continued to split his time between regal duties and the

"ELIZABETH WAS BEGINNING TO SHOW SIGNS OF A SENSE OF DUTY WHILE MARGARET'S HIGH SPIRITS WERE INCREASINGLY CLEAR"

fast life that was beginning to cause his family grave concerns. Their London home became well known as the setting for important dinner parties, which attracted guests from all walks of life. JM Barrie and Rudyard Kipling both dined there, as did leading politicians Ramsay MacDonald and Stanley Baldwin. The couple were also taking on more patronages and an extensive diary of public engagements and tours. Much of the behind-the-scenes work for those events went on at their London residence, all while Lillibet and Margot ran through its corridors chasing their pet dogs and causing mischief.

But differences between the sisters were already starting to appear. Elizabeth was beginning to show signs of a sense of duty while Margaret's high spirits were increasingly clear. Marion Crawford said later that what her employers had really wanted for their daughters was "a happy childhood, with lots of pleasant memories stored up against the days that might come out". In 1936, those dark days finally arrived.

The happy home was plunged into mourning on 20 January that year when King George V died at the age of 71. The duke of York - now heir to the throne - and his wife found themselves taking on even more high-profile engagements. However, on the Continent, the new king, Edward VIII, was entertaining his American lover, Wallis Simpson. By the time the Yorks returned to their London home after their summer holidays, it became increasingly clear that a crisis was developing.

It was within the walls of their townhouse they had come to love that Bertie and Elizabeth first contemplated the prospect of Edward's abdication. When the king finally did give up his throne on 11 December 1936, their happy home finally had to be abandoned.

The new king and queen moved with their daughters to Buckingham Palace, and 145 Piccadilly was packed up. Soon after its royal residents left, the building was no more. War came quickly and in the early months, the former regal home was used as an office for a relief fund. But on 7 October 1940, during the Blitz, a highly explosive bomb fell on it, causing extensive damage. An air warden's report noted that a caretaker and his family had been found among the wreckage. 145 Piccadilly was gone. In the late 1960s, plans were drawn up for a luxury hotel on the site with the new building opening in 1975.

But while the house itself is gone, its memories live on. It had been a happy base for a young couple and their daughters, and the joy they found in one another would end up being seen on a world stage as Bertie and Elizabeth took the throne and the 'Us Four' that had begun with its happy life at 145 Piccadilly became the foundation of a new royal family.

Princess Elizabeth spent hours playing in the gardens of 145 Piccadilly with her pet dogs

The end of an era - a 'to let' sign went up over 145 Piccadilly as its royal residents moved into Buckingham Palace following the accession of King George VI

TO TEACH A QUEEN

An heir's education has always been a serious matter, but Elizabeth's parents decided to prioritise a happy childhood over preparation for the daunting task of ruling

Throughout history, the education of the heir to the throne has always been a matter of paramount importance, with huge amounts of attention paid to ensuring that the heir in question receives not just the best education possibl,e but also a proper preparation for the gruelling task ahead.

In the 16th century, the children of Henry VIII had been provided with extraordinarily thorough educations that encompassed several languages as well as mathematics, philosophy and theology. In the 19th century, Queen Victoria and Prince Albert had taken an intense interest in the training of their eldest son, Bertie, Prince of Wales, creating a strict educational regimen that had covered a broad range of subjects and ensured that their son was, albeit rather unwillingly, one of the best educated monarchs ever to succeed to the British throne.

Unfortunately, Bertie's experience had been such a miserable one that he had decided not to repeat it when it came to his own children, whose own education was relatively unremarkable and in some respects rather desultory considering their station. To the horror of Queen Victoria, both of her eldest grandsons, Prince Albert Victor and Prince George, who would succeed as George V in 1911, struggled to speak any languages other than English, and attempts to force them to improve their linguistic skills were destined to

fail horribly. In contrast, George's wife, Mary, was exceptionally well educated and was able to speak not just French and German but also some Italian, thanks to a year spent in Florence as a young woman. It was due to her that the next generation of royals, which included her sons Edward VIII and George VI, was rather better educated.

When Mary's granddaughter Elizabeth was born in April 1926, she was not expected to ever sit on the throne. Her father's elder brother, David, Prince of Wales, was still only in his early 30s and although he had not yet married, it was anticipated that he would do so very soon and then commence producing his own brood. Thus, Elizabeth's parents felt no great pressure to impose a rigorous education upon their daughter, preferring instead to emulate the cheerfully undemanding upbringing that her mother, the duchess of York, had enjoyed as the youngest daughter of a Scottish earl.

In common with other upper-class girls of the time, the duchess of York had, for the most part, been educated at home by governesses, who taught her French and some German and encouraged an early passion for history. Although some girls were sent to boarding school, it was still considered the norm for them to be educated at home, while their brothers, who were deemed more in need of a proper education, were sent away to school, followed by university.

When Queen Mary expressed some concern about the education of Elizabeth and her younger sister, Margaret – who was born in 1930 but didn't join her in the schoolroom until the age of seven – the duchess of York airily dismissed her worries by reminding her that her own parents had considered it far more important to prepare their daughters to make good marriages, and that this gamble had definitely paid off, as "I and my sisters all married well, some of us very well".

As far as the duchess was concerned, there was no reason for her own daughters to be educated any differently, especially as it was so unlikely that either of them would be succeeding to the throne. They were instead almost certainly destined to marry into the upper echelons of the aristocracy, where they would be fully employed running great houses, overseeing huge households and raising their own children.

As soon as she was born, Elizabeth, who would be known as 'Lilibet' in tribute to her initial attempts to pronounce her own name, was consigned to the devoted care of her mother's old nanny, the redoubtable Clara Knight, known as 'Allah' by her young charges, who adored her. Allah was the archetypical formidable British nanny, who ran the nursery with a strict attention to detail, ensuring that every moment of Elizabeth's day was fully accounted for and that there were no opportunities for

© Getty

Art was a favourite pastime of both of the sisters, although neither had any particular talent

idleness, fidgeting or bad behaviour. Meals were plain and wholesome, toys were played with one at a time and then carefully put away, there was a daily walk whatever the weather, and the highlight of every day was the precious hour spent downstairs with her parents every evening before she was whisked away to bed.

However, although Allah ruled the nursery, it was the duchess of York herself who taught Elizabeth to read and encouraged her to embark on a lifelong love of books, which had the additional benefit of enabling her to remedy any deficiencies in her education. "I read quite quickly now," Elizabeth would tell the author JK Rowling many years later. "I have to read a lot."

But when her younger sister, Margaret, was born, Allah took charge of the new baby while little Elizabeth was passed to the care of a new nanny, Margaret 'Bobo' MacDonald, who would remain with her for the rest of her life as dresser and confidante, touchingly always referring to

"SHE WAS TAKEN ABACK BY HOW UNDEMANDING THE ROYAL FAMILY WERE"

Elizabeth as her 'little lady' even after she had become queen.

In 1933, when Elizabeth was seven years old, the York nursery upstairs in their townhouse at 145 Piccadilly was joined by a bright new Scottish governess, Marion Crawford, who was quickly nicknamed 'Crawfie' by her charges. She would supervise the education of the two princesses, aided by a series of tutors for French, dancing, music and art - all of which were considered essential accomplishments for upper-class girls.

Crawfie was rather taken aback by how undemanding the royal family were about her charges' educations, writing later in her controversial book *The Little Princesses* that "no one ever had employers who interfered so little". She confided that their gruff grandfather, who

adored Elizabeth and treated her with a warm-hearted affection that he had rarely shown to his own children, had cornered her in order to demand: "For goodness sake, teach Margaret and Lilibet a decent hand, that's all I ask of you." George V's own handwriting was execrable, while his terrible spelling caused him much embarrassment over the years, and he had clearly come to the conclusion that while other educational deficiencies could always be overlooked or remedied, legible handwriting was an essential life skill that required extra attention.

However, his wife, Queen Mary, was rather more exacting and insisted that there should be particular emphasis on the teaching of geography and history, which she believed were essential topics for a potential future monarch. To assist in

©Getty

30

Princess Elizabeth was cared for from birth by her mother's formidable but kind-hearted old nanny, Clara Knight, known to her adoring charges as 'Allah'

MARION CRAWFORD

The two princesses adored their Scottish governess, but their love quickly turned to disdain when she broke their trust

Born into an ordinary family in Gatehead, East Ayrshire, in June 1909, Marion Crawford trained as a teacher after leaving school before studying to become a child psychologist, taking nannying jobs in order to supplement her income. When she joined the York household in spring 1932, she was initially supposed to stay for just a month but was such a success that the position was made permanent and she remained with the family for 17 years.

When she finally retired after Princess Elizabeth's marriage in November 1947, Crawford was given Nottingham Cottage at Kensington Palace as a home as a mark of the royal family's appreciation. Shortly afterwards, she was contacted by an American magazine, which offered to commission articles about the two princesses and their education. Pressured by her new husband who was keen to capitalise on her connection with royalty, she agreed to do write the articles nder her own name, despite the disapproval of her former employers. In 1950, the articles were followed by a book, *The Little Princesses*, which was an international bestseller but resulted in Crawford's complete ostracism by the royal family and the loss of her cottage. When she died in 1980 there was no acknowledgement from the royal family, and even many years later, the expression 'doing a Crawfie' was used by the family as code for anyone who betrayed their confidence.

this worthy enterprise, she accompanied both of her granddaughters on regular visits to museums, art galleries and other sites of historical significance around London.

Although Crawfie did her best to give her charges as broad an education as possible, she was defeated by the fact that she was only able to teach Elizabeth for one and a half hours every morning, and even that precious time, which was not nearly enough for a bright and curious child of seven, was constantly interrupted. The rest of the day was taken up with meals, nap time and plenty of playing outside - which in the

countryside involved riding lessons on her beloved Shetland pony, Peggy, a fourth birthday present from her doting grandfather, and one that ignited a lifelong passion for horses.

Although the duke of York was second in line to the throne, he nonetheless hoped that his daughters would be free to enjoy their carefree, happy existence for several years to come - only to be disappointed when his father died in January 1936 and his brother succeeded the throne as Edward VIII. If the new king had also been happily married and father to a brood of promising children then the diffident duke, who had absolutely no desire to one day become king - even if he was doubtless well aware that both of his parents had hoped that the crown would one day come to him - would have felt much more comfortable. However, his brother was still very much enjoying the hectic, louche existence of a wealthy bachelor prince. The only signs he showed of wanting to settle down were with Wallis Simpson, a divorcée of whom Parliament and the royal family thoroughly disapproved.

There was some talk at this time of sending Elizabeth to school, but her parents' determination to keep her at home and provide her with a happy childhood persevered and the lessons with Crawfie continued. As Elizabeth got older, more time was devoted to her lessons, and they covered an increasingly broad range of subjects, with poetry, literature and grammar being added to history and geography, although unfortunately Crawfie turned out to be unequal to the task of teaching maths at any advanced level.

Special tutors were brought in to teach the princesses dancing, music and French, although early French lessons did not always go well, with

Although her education was rather patchy, Princess Elizabeth managed to develop a lifelong love of reading

Marion Crawford frequently took her charges on excursions in London, even on the Tube

the small Elizabeth even upturning a pot of ink over own head during one particularly frustrating lesson. Such outbursts were rare, though, as right from the start, Elizabeth was a conscientious, quiet and unusually well-behaved child - unlike her sister, who was wilful, naughty and high spirited. Music lessons were much more popular, with Margaret showing particular talent and becoming an exceptionally gifted pianist.

As the two sisters shared their lessons and never had any classmates or exams, they were relieved of the pressure of competing with other children of the same age. However, at the same time they had no real way to assess their progress, which left them feeling insecure about their intellectual abilities, despite the fact that their parents were so cheerfully unconcerned about the matter. The possibility of one day going to university was almost certainly never mentioned, even though at the time, an increasing numbers of young women were going into higher education, with the result that much later in life Elizabeth would ruefully comment that she did not believe that she and her sister would have succeeded in getting places at university anyway.

Whatever hopes the duke and duchess of York might have had that their daughters would enjoy a normal, carefree existence were finally shattered towards the end of 1936 when Edward VIII signalled his intention to marry his mistress, Wallis Simpson, who had recently divorced for the second time. The resulting crisis ended with the king's abdication in December, less than a year after he had succeeded to the throne, and the very unwilling succession of Elizabeth's father, who took the name George VI, while his eldest daughter became heir presumptive to the throne. The new royal family moved into Buckingham Palace within a few weeks, with Elizabeth and her sister being assigned a very prettily decorated suite of rooms overlooking the Mall, with tall windows from which the two

Princess Margaret joined her sister in the schoolroom at the age of seven, which she later felt was too late as she regretted not having more of an education

"THEY WERE RELIEVED OF THE PRESSURE OF COMPETING"

princesses could wistfully watch people go about their business down below.

Their lessons with Crawfie continued as normal but the new king's sense that he had been ill-prepared for the daunting task ahead of him made him determined to ensure that his own heir should be better equipped when her

time came. To this end, in 1938 he arranged that Elizabeth should travel to Windsor twice a week in order to take special private lessons in constitutional history with the Vice-Provost of Eton College, Henry Marten. While Crawfie, who acted as chaperone, sat in the corner quietly reading, Marten taught his young pupil about

Princess Elizabeth's daily routine involved more time playing outside than actual lessons

PRINCESS ELIZABETH'S DAILY ROUTINE

The duchess of York wanted her children's upbringing to be as happy and carefree as her own

The day would start early with breakfast in the nursery and then the two princesses were taken downstairs to their parents' bedroom for 'high jinks' and private family time before the duke and duchess had to go about their day, which often took them out of the house until evening, and the girls went through to their schoolroom, which was next to their mother's bedroom. Lessons, which were frequently interrupted

by visits from dentists, doctors, dressmakers and photographers, would take place between 9.30 and 11am, when they stopped for a snack and an hour of playing the garden, until midday when they had their nap, followed by an hour of Crawfie reading aloud, preferably from a book about animals. If their parents were home, the princesses had lunch with them before spending the rest of the day playing. They also had dancing

and music lessons in the afternoon before they were taken downstairs to spend an hour with their mother before they had supper, followed by their daily bath, which the duke and duchess usually made a point of attending and which usually involved a lot of splashing and messing around. When the two little girls went to bed, they would call their goodnights to their parents from the top of the stairs.

Princess Elizabeth adored her father's elder brother, the future Edward VIII, but their relationship became distant as she got older

Although Princess Elizabeth had a reputation of being a solemn, quiet and shy child, she was also cheerful and good natured

Princess Elizabeth learned to ride at an early age on a Shetland pony given to her by her grandfather George V; it was to be the first of many horses

history, government and the often confusing Constitution of the United Kingdom, the rules and legislation that determine the governance of the nation that she would one day reign over.

Although the subject matter was often extremely dry and she was occasionally daunted by the reading material, which included weighty tomes about English social history, law and politics, Elizabeth nonetheless enjoyed her sessions with Marten thanks to his engaging and gregarious manner. The chief cornerstone of the curriculum were the three volumes of Sir William Anson's *The Law and Custom of the Constitution*, which she dutifully read while taking notes and underlining the most significant passages, particularly those that related to her own future role. Gruelling and tedious though these studies must on occasion have been, they served her well as in later life; several of Elizabeth's prime ministers would be deeply impressed by her grasp of the Constitution.

Shortly after World War II broke out in 1939, the two princesses and their household moved to the relative safety of Windsor Castle, where they

were to remain until the end of the war in 1945, often only seeing their parents at weekends. While at Windsor, their education continued as usual, with Elizabeth still having her lessons with Henry Marten, while the rest of the curriculum was, as always, covered by Crawfie, a French teacher, Mrs Montaudon-Smith, and dance and music tutors. Elizabeth supplemented all of this with her own private reading of books in the expansive royal library as well as avid readings of the weekly tabloid, *The Children's Newspaper*, subtitled 'The Story of the World Today for the Men and Women of Tomorrow', to which Crawfie had subscribed Elizabeth, hoping that it would increase her awareness and understanding of current affairs.

Fearing that her granddaughters were woefully ignorant about art, Queen Mary, who had become passionately interested in art history during her youthful sojourn in Florence, arranged for precious paintings from the Royal Collection to be placed on an easel in their schoolroom. She took it upon herself to ensure that they were educated about the art treasures that hung on the

walls of the royal palaces and castles around the United Kingdom.

In 1942, Elizabeth's education was given a further veneer of sophistication when Vicomtesse Marie-Antoinette de Bellaigue joined the household in Windsor in order to give the two princesses lessons in French language and history, as well as an understanding of other nations and their customs. Under Madame de Bellaigue's directions, only French was spoken at mealtimes and the two girls quickly increased their fluency, while at the same time acquiring a little bit of French polish.

Elizabeth's education was formally considered to be at an end when she turned 18 in 1944, and although it had not been as rigorous as perhaps it should have been, especially when compared to that of past heirs to the throne, still her parents were very satisfied with how she had turned out. Any deficiencies were more than compensated for by her sensible, self-possessed manner, deep dedication to duty, and poise - essential qualities for a future queen.

THE UNEXPECTED HEIR

Despite being born third in line to the throne, Princess Elizabeth of York's transformation into a queen-in-waiting came as a shock to many

Words **June Woolerton**

The lives of George VI and his elder daughter, Elizabeth, changed forever on 10 December 1936 when the abdication transformed them into king and heir

Queen Mary, already a major influence on her granddaughter, took a leading role in Elizabeth's life once she became heir

King George V made no secret of the desperation he sometimes felt over his heir, the man who would briefly reign as Edward VIII. The founder of the House of Windsor once declared he hoped his eldest son would "never marry and have children and that nothing will stand between Bertie and Lilibet and the throne". He could have had no idea of how dramatically his wish would come true. Within a year of George V's death, Edward

VIII had given up his crown for love, leaving Bertie as King George VI and Lilibet as Princess Elizabeth, the unexpected heir to the throne.

It was a role no one had expected her to take on when she was born. As the first child of Albert and Elizabeth, Duke and Duchess of York, she was a celebrated royal baby, but one expected to fade into regal obscurity as her parents had more children and her uncle provided the House of Windsor with a suitable bride and a nursery of potential heirs.

When she welcomed a sister, Margaret Rose, in 1930, Elizabeth's situation changed subtly.

The duchess of York had given birth to both her children by Caesarean section, and medical wisdom at the time counselled against a third pregnancy. Lilibet was now highly unlikely to be deposed in the pecking order by a baby brother. Although the smart money was on her uncle having a family of his own, Lilibet was sure of remaining her father's heir. Bertie had no desire to be king and even less inkling to place the responsibility of monarchy on his beloved daughter's shoulders, but George V and Queen Mary began to take a keener interest in the

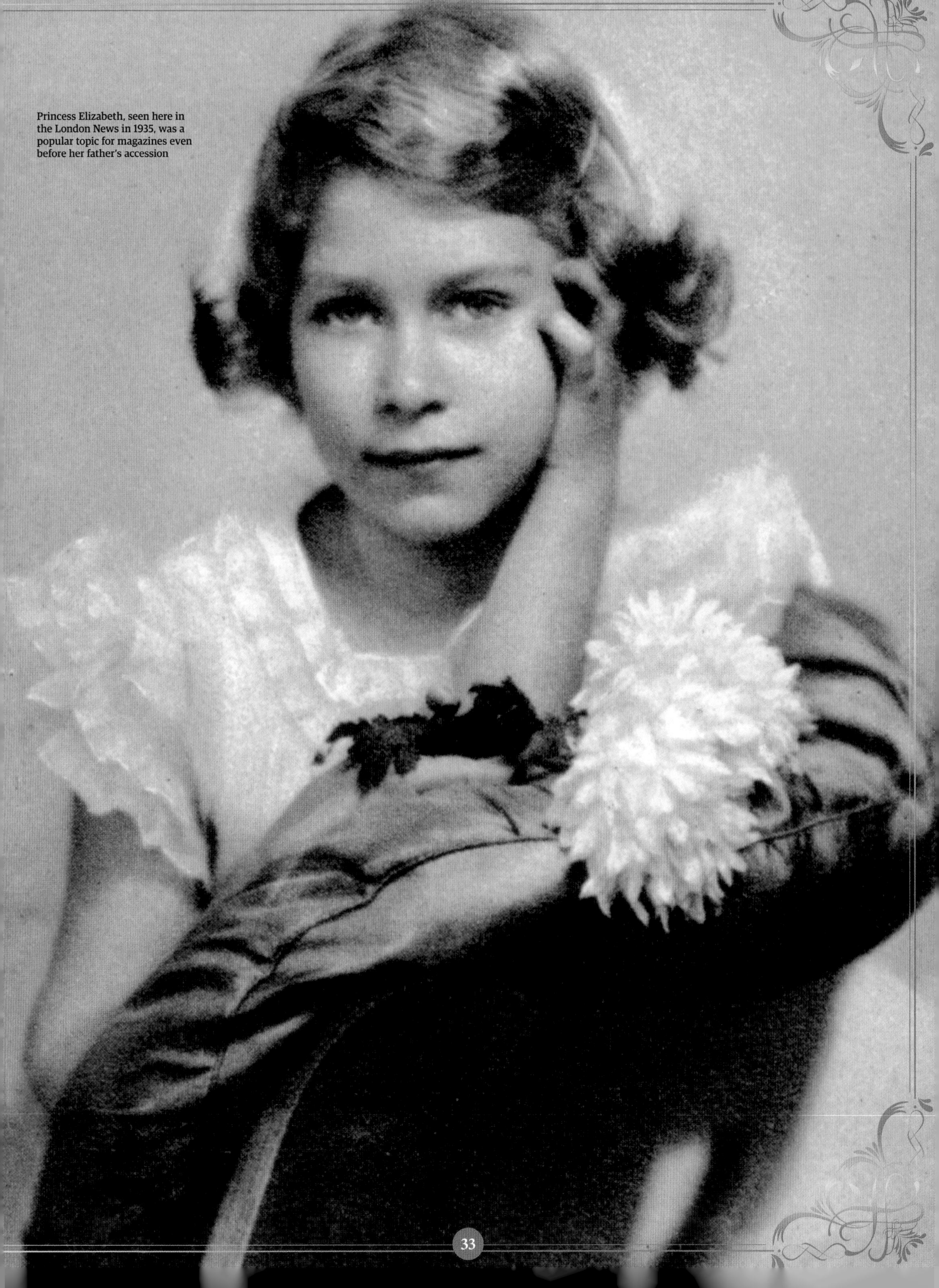

Princess Elizabeth, seen here in the London News in 1935, was a popular topic for magazines even before her father's accession

SOUVENIR of the CORONATION of KING GEORGE VI & QUEEN ELIZABETH

CROWNED 12th MAY 1937. GOD BLESS THEM

INDIA · CANADA · NEW ZEALAND · S. AFRICA · AUSTRALIA · BRITISH POSSESSIONS

education of their granddaughter, just in case her destiny should change.

The loss of King George V, who she called 'Grandpa England', was a heavy blow for Elizabeth, who was just nine when he died at Sandringham House, Norfolk, following a short illness on 20 January 1936. He had been a major influence and, as a baby, she had spent months with him and Queen Mary while her parents went on a tour of Australia. But while she mourned, her uncle was already showing signs of the impetuous nature and illicit passion that would lead him to abandon his throne. While Lilibet, Margaret and their parents supported the grieving Queen Mary, the new Edward VIII had gone against tradition and travelled to London to hear his own proclamation as king with an American friend, Wallis Simpson, at his side.

Their relationship had remained hidden from the wider British public but was well known in Edward's most intimate circles. Wallis had been introduced to his parents and his brothers, but while the nature of their bond was clear, she was outwardly the wife of another of his friends, Ernest Simpson. Furthermore, Ernest was her second husband. There were

also rumours of salacious episodes during her life overseas to contend with, and concerns over the hold she exerted on the new king. Perhaps most troubling were reports of her links with members of the Nazi Party in Germany. Wallis was far from an ideal partner for a king, but the new monarch steadfastly set his heart on making her his queen.

While Mrs Simpson lurked in the shadows of an obscurity willingly provided by the British press, the new king basked in the glory of public adulation. Edward had always been popular. He was glamorous and the perfect modern antidote to the stuffy reign of his strict father. He also had a knack of producing the perfect soundbite. As Prince of Wales he had made a habit of travelling to areas badly hit by the economic woes of the late 1920s and early 1930s. His declarations that "something must be done" as he walked, in his always fashionable clothes, among the grim streets that other royals eschewed had turned him into the public's darling. It also gave him a sense of security in the summer of 1936.

As he toured Europe with Wallis, Edward became ever more convinced they would soon be husband and wife. Elizabeth, meanwhile, was spending her holidays at Glamis, her mother's ancestral home in Scotland. There she enjoyed the

EXTRA

FOR CLASSIFIED PHONE RICHMOND 4141

Only Los Angeles Newspaper With All Leading News Services — Associated Press, International News, United Press, Dow-Jones

LOS ANGELES EVENING **HERALD Express** AN INDEPENDENT NEWSPAPER

LATEST NEWS

The Evening Herald and Express Grows Just Like Los Angeles

VOL. LXVI THREE CENTS · THURSDAY, DECEMBER 10, 1936 · THREE CENTS · NO. 222

EDWARD ABDICATES; BROTHER TO BE KING

Baldwin Tells Inside Details of Meetings With Edward

Text of Abdication Message

By Associated Press

RULER GIVES UP THRONE FOR LOVE OF MRS. SIMPSON

Edward VIII leads his younger brother, the future George VI, out for Trooping the Colour in 1936

same carefree and relaxed upbringing that marked her early childhood with Margaret. The pair, unlike other royal children, weren't confined to one wing of their latest residence. Instead, they had the run of the house as well as its grounds and indulged their passions, including playing with their pet dogs and horse riding, unaware that a constitutional crisis was looming.

Life hadn't changed that much for them since the loss of Grandpa England. While their father was now heir to the throne and had been at his brother's side at major events like Trooping the Colour, the York family had carried on as before. The duke and duchess took on public engagements while their daughters spent their mornings learning and their afternoons with friends in the garden of their London home. Albert had none of his brother's glamour, wit or public charm, but his undoubted sense of duty had won him fans of his own. His wife was even more popular, but they remained supporting acts in the royal family.

However, in the autumn of 1936, both began to sense that an enormous change was underfoot as rumours swept the upper classes of London that the king was about to marry. Wallis Simpson filed for divorce in October and soon afterwards Edward summoned Prime Minister Stanley Baldwin to Buckingham Palace to inform him he had chosen his queen. Baldwin explained that a wedding was out of the question due to Simpson's status as a divorcée, but the new king was undeterred.

Discussions began about a morganatic marriage, which would stop Wallis becoming queen and bestow on her a courtesy title instead, but opposition to any form of union began to grow. The British press finally broke their silence at the

> "WALLIS WAS FAR FROM AN IDEAL PARTNER FOR A KING, BUT EDWARD SET HIS HEART ON HER"

LILIBET'S CORONATION OBSESSION

While her father was daunted by the prospect of his coronation, Princess Elizabeth loved every moment of the historic day

Princess Elizabeth had been taught from an early age to love history by her grandmother, Queen Mary. But as she prepared to attend her father's coronation, as heir to the throne, her family encouraged her passion even further. Lilibet leapt at the chance to absorb the past.

She delighted in a book her father had made for her, explaining the whole spectacle in pictures. Queen Mary talked to her about past coronations and found a guide to previous ceremonies for her to study. Elizabeth also studied the names and roles of all the dignitaries involved in this ancient tradition and learned them by heart.

On the day itself, she arrived at Westminster Abbey in a white dress and coronet, happily greeting those waiting for her. Despite her proximity to the crown she had no formal role in the ceremony and watched it unfold alongside her grandmother and her little sister, Margaret, who had showed off until she'd been allowed to wear an outfit identical to Elizabeth's. The elder sister watched the event solemnly, absorbing every detail. Days later she wrote her own version of the historic moment in a letter that is still kept in the Royal Archives.

Elizabeth arrived at her parents' coronation on 12 May 1937 as a young queen-in-waiting

Princess Elizabeth showed remarkable composure during the coronation of her father and seemed to relish greeting the huge crowds afterwards

start of December 1936 when reports appeared of a speech by the bishop of Bradford, asking for "divine grace" for the king. The crisis escalated rapidly as papers carried headlines stating that Edward VIII was about to marry Mrs Simpson. Behind palace doors, the king was told by his politicians that he had to give up his lover or his throne.

Lilibet remained unaware of the drama, perhaps because her own father was also being left out of discussions. For several crucial days, starting on 3 December 1936, Bertie wasn't able to see his brother, who kept delaying meetings between them. Some of Edward's associates put it down to his own anxiety about a situation that was slipping from his control.

However, intense discussions were going on about Bertie's suitability to succeed to the throne, with some royal advisors concerned that his heir was a princess. Female heirs were a rarity, both in British history and in contemporary Europe, where just one princess stood in line to inherit a throne and only because she had no brothers. Some continental monarchies still barred women and their descendants from succeeding at all, and there was concern among the politicians involved in the abdication crisis about whether a female heir would further destabilise a throne set to endure a massive shock.

Elizabeth in one of the photo sessions her mother organised before the abdication to underline the homely nature of the House of Windsor

The fact he had no son to succeed him wasn't the only reason some in the inner circles of the royal family questioned whether the duke of York should take the crown if his brother gave it up. Bertie was notoriously shy and had worked hard to overcome a stammer that had left him struggling to speak at times. He became frustrated at what he perceived to be his failings and privately had been known to fly into rages as his unhappiness got the better of him. He was also known to dread the prospect of becoming king, and there were fears that this could further exacerbate his anxiety and his stutter.

On paper, his youngest surviving brother, George, seemed a much better candidate. The young duke of Kent was handsome, suave and every bit as charming as Edward. He also had a son. The baby prince had been born in 1935 and was about to get a sibling as the duke's wife, Marina, part of the Greek royal family, was days away from delivering their second child. But George also had a wayward past. When Bertie finally met his big brother on 7 December 1936, he was told the abdication would take place imminently and he would become king within days.

When Edward VIII signed away his empire on 10 December, Princess Elizabeth was at home with her mother and sister. The new king returned to the family house at 145 Piccadilly later that evening,

© Getty, Alamy

Princess Elizabeth went from royal curiosity to constitutional necessity in the time it took her uncle to sign the abdication papers

Princess Elizabeth was already being introduced to life in the public eye by her parents before the abdication became a reality

THE COUSIN WHO WAS ALMOST KING

Elizabeth's path to the throne was almost blocked by a baby boy nine years her junior

Edward, Duke of Kent, was always a loyal supporter of his cousin during her long reign as Queen Elizabeth II. But for a few days before the abdication, he was the prince who almost stole her crown. He was just a baby at the time.

Edward George Nicholas Paul Patrick was born on 9 October 1935, just months before the death of King George V. His father was the king's youngest surviving son, George, Duke of Kent, while his mother was the popular Princess Marina of Greece and Denmark.

Politicians and courtiers already worried by the damage the abdication would do to the monarchy became even more alarmed at the prospect of installing a girl as heir to the throne. A baby prince was far more appealing. Not only was he a boy, but he also had a lot more blue blood than Lilibet, whose maternal grandparents were a mere earl and countess compared to the Russian grand duchess and Greek prince from whom Edward was descended.

Princess Elizabeth, then nine, looks at her baby cousin, Prince Edward, who came close to being named heir in her place

In the end, the pressure of tradition won out and Edward VIII was succeeded by Lilibet's father, who had been heir throughout the short reign. Edward and the queen he almost displaced remained close, and he continued to carry out royal duties for her well into his 80s.

"GEORGE VI NOW BEGAN TO INTRODUCE HIS HEIR TO THE DAILY PROCESSES OF RULING"

caught on camera as he stared into the distance, pale and clearly shaken. The reality of their new lives became even clearer the following day when George VI, as he was now to be known, left for his Accession Council at St James' Palace. Years later, Elizabeth's nanny revealed how that historic morning had unfolded. Marion Crawford wrote that the new heir to the throne and her sister had run to their father as he left and hugged him, but when he returned "both girls swept him a beautiful curtsey".

Elizabeth was now a queen-in-waiting, but the ten-year-old couldn't claim many of the ancient titles that belonged to the first in line. As a girl, she would be known as heiress presumptive rather than assumptive as she could still be overtaken should her father ever have a son. She would also remain Princess Elizabeth. The title of Prince of Wales could only be given to a monarch's eldest surviving son, while the even older honour of duke of Cornwall was also off limits to daughters.

But a stark reminder of her new life arrived soon afterwards. Lilibet and Margaret saw a letter in the hallway addressed to 'Her Majesty the Queen'. After realising it was for their mother, Margaret asked her older sister if that would be her title one day too. "Some day," came the reply.

Although it seemed a long way off, preparations for that day began almost as soon as George VI took the throne. Queen Mary, who had always encouraged her grandchildren to read history books, now took an even deeper interest in the education of the ten-year-old princess. She worked closely with her tutors on what should be taught to the young monarch-in-waiting, while arrangements were made for Elizabeth to take lessons in constitutional history.

George VI was also deeply aware of the change in his daughter's status. He himself had never been trained to be king, but he now began to introduce his heir slowly to the daily processes of ruling, from the red boxes containing government papers to the meetings and audiences that would dominate both their lives. Elizabeth was a willing student; she had always been the more studious and dutiful of the two York princesses, and now as her new

role began she applied herself to performing it. She listened avidly to descriptions of what would happen at the coronation, and there were few complaints as her lessons lengthened as her family began the process of producing a queen regnant.

She also took the changes to her day-to-day life in her stride. She and Margaret were uprooted from their happy home in Piccadilly as they moved to Buckingham Palace. They inevitably saw less of their parents, who both had new roles to fulfil, and they also had to learn to live without the presence of their uncle. David, as Edward VIII had always been known to family, had been a frequent visitor to the York house. Now he was living in France as the duke of Windsor, and the new regime had decided it would be better if he stayed away.

Instead, he watched from a distance as his brother ruled the kingdom he had been born to inherit while his niece prepared to succeed to the crown. He saw a tight family unit intent on succeeding, for while neither George VI nor Elizabeth ever wanted to rule, they determined to do it as well as they could now that their unexpected successions had been assured.

Elizabeth stands proudly in front of well-maintained truck during her ATS training

WHAT DID YOU DO IN THE WAR, MA'AM?

Changing spark plugs, enduring the ominous drone of enemy aircraft passing overhead, performing duties usually placed on much older shoulders - the teenage Princess Elizabeth strode through it all with extraordinary poise and courage

Words **Jon Wright**

Winston Churchill's private secretary, Jock Colville, was "embarrassed by the sloppy sentiment [the Princess Elizabeth] had been made to express", but had found "her voice most impressive". Colville was commenting upon Elizabeth's Children's Hour radio address, broadcast on 13 October 1940 and, to be fair, the speech did tug rather heavily on the heart strings. Then again, perhaps that was precisely what an audience of children yearned to hear at such a frightening time.

"Thousands of you in this country have had to leave your homes and be separated from your fathers and mothers," Elizabeth began. "My sister Margaret Rose and I feel so much for you as we know from experience what it means to be away from those we love most of all." The evacuees, alongside all the children who had remained at

home, should feel proud: "We are trying to do all we can to help our gallant sailors, soldiers and airmen, and we are trying, too, to bear our own share of the danger and sadness of war."

It's important to stress just how unusual this broadcast was. 14-year-old members of the British royal family were not in the habit of making speeches across the airwaves. But times had changed. Britain was at war and Elizabeth turned out to be one of the royal family's greatest assets. More than that, her commitment to the cause seems to have been profound and utterly genuine.

What to do with the children?
The few months before the outbreak of hostilities had been particularly exciting for Princess Elizabeth. She became the first royal to make a transatlantic phone call (to

her father, who was away on state business in Canada) and a trip to the Naval College at Dartmouth resulted in Elizabeth's first, rather charming encounter with some chap named Philip Mountbatten. As soon as war began, however, the issue of the children's safety became an urgent matter.

Lord Hailsham suggested sending Elizabeth and Margaret to Canada, but the queen was having none of it. "The children won't go without me," she explained, "I won't leave without the king. And the king will never leave." A short stay at Balmoral was followed by Christmas at the Sandringham estate, but by February 1940, Windsor had emerged as the least risky long-term solution. Up to June 1940, the children were billeted in the cosy Royal Lodge but with Germany's menacing inroads on the Continent - overrunning Belgium, Holland and France - the princesses were moved into the castle, with its sturdy walls and deep basements. At this stage, the king and queen typically stayed at Buckingham Palace during the week, with weekends spent at Windsor. When the bombing of London intensified during the autumn of October 1940, schedules had to change. The royal couple would now travel up to London for the day's work but be back to the safety of Windsor by nightfall.

Spending one's days ensconced in a well-appointed Berkshire castle may not sound like the toughest of wickets, but Windsor had changed. The glitzy porcelain and chandeliers had been packed away, glass-fronted cabinets had been turned to face the walls, and the castle had transformed into a gloomy labyrinth of dust sheets and black-out curtains. The queen's cousin Margaret Rhodes lamented how Windsor "had returned to its original role as a fortress": an impression only enhanced by the arrival of barbed-wire-covered pill-boxes in the grounds or the sight of nightly patrols heading off to ensure that no pesky Germans had parachuted into Windsor Great Park.

Routines were maintained as well as possible, of course. Elizabeth soldiered on with her lessons: history from the likeable Henry Marten, vice-provost of Eton; French and dancing from the exiled Marie-Antoinette de Bellaigue; and regular tips on protocol and deportment from the king's mother, Queen Mary. There was space for fun, too. A new Girl Guides troop was established, with Elizabeth and Margaret earning their badges alongside local

The king and queen inspect the damage caused by a direct hit on Buckingham Palace in 1940

Queen Wilhelmina of the Netherlands, one of several exiled crowned heads who fetched up in wartime Britain in 1940

schoolchildren and East End evacuees who, rather pleasingly, showed little interest in the princesses' lofty social status. During the Christmas season, wherever the family found itself, pantomimes became de rigueur. The first, in 1940, starred Margaret as Cinderella with Elizabeth as a rather diffident Prince Charming. Ticket prices were steep - seven-and-sixpence for the best seats - but the proceeds all went to the queen's Wool Fund. The run of yearly shows - including a memorable *Aladdin* in 1943 - raised more than £800 in total. When the atmosphere became too stifling, it was always possible to arrange a getaway to the bracing air of Balmoral and, while having Grenadier Guards patrolling Windsor was perhaps a little

"THEY CAN'T GET ON WITHOUT US"

The famous slogan was absolutely accurate: the ATS made an incalculable contribution to the war effort, even if the dreams of women playing a much more substantial role in the post-war economy were quickly dashed

By the time Elizabeth donned her ATS uniform, the service was handling a bewildering array of tasks: working as fitters, wireless operators, electricians, carpenters and draughtswomen. Some jobs were highly technical, such as the cinetheodolite operators who recorded the chaps' efforts at gun practice and applied mathematical wizardry to calculate trajectories and impact. Some jobs took real guts, not least work on anti-aircraft batteries, where women served alongside men, though without the satisfaction of firing the guns.

As Frederick Pile commented at the time, "there was a good deal of muddled thinking which was prepared to allow women to do anything to kill the enemy except actually pull the

trigger". Lazy assumptions about female sensibilities died hard. Those ATS members who travelled to Egypt spent, according to an official publication, an inordinate amount of time lapping up the "traditional glories of the east" and "never tire of looking at the pyramids and the Nile or shopping in the bazaars".

The successful 1943 film *The Gentle Sex* paints a fond portrait of the ATS but ends with narration by Leslie Howard that is still cringeworthy almost 80 years later: "Well there they are, the women. Our sweethearts, sisters, mothers, daughters. Let's give in at last and admit we're really proud of you. You strange, wonderful, incalculable creatures." Small wonder that a patriarchal economic culture returned with a thud as soon war ended.

Who could resist? An ATS recruitment brochure from 1940

A downed Messerschmitt Bf 109E-1 on display outside Windsor Castle in 1944

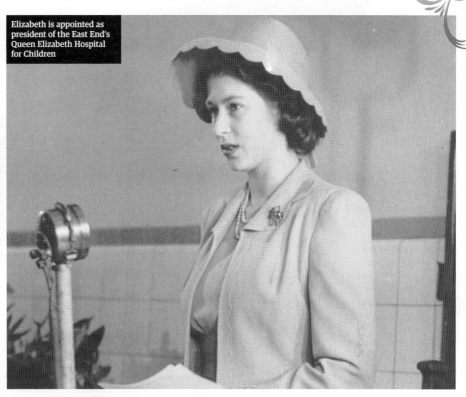

Elizabeth is appointed as president of the East End's Queen Elizabeth Hospital for Children

"BUCKINGHAM PALACE CERTAINLY DID NOT GO UNSCATHED, BEING ATTACKED 16 TIMES"

On a visit to Windsor in June 1941, Peter enjoyed a post-breakfast treat courtesy of Elizabeth: she "took me on a tour of the castle with its huge ramparts and interminable corridors" followed by a walk, with Margaret and the dogs in tow, around the grounds. Peter found them to be "charming young girls."

The bombs were another dead giveaway that a war was being waged. Buckingham Palace certainly did not go unscathed, being attacked 16 times and suffering nine direct hits. The scariest moment came on 13 September 1940. A single German plane headed straight down the Mall in broad daylight and let loose its payload. One bomb exploded just 30 yards from where the king was working: a shockingly narrow escape. Windsor also saw its share of the action and, while no major damage was inflicted, 300 bombs fell in the grounds during the war.

Almost as terrifying was the nighttime scurrying to the castle's basements. Margaret well remembered the routine: "the siren would go", she and her sister would be woken and dressed, and "we would be set off on the long trot down the corridor, down the stairs... and then down the cold stone steps to this shelter which lies at the bottom of the towers". The queen confessed to Queen Mary that "I am afraid that Windsor is not really a good place for them, the noise of guns is heavy and then of course there have been so many bombs dropped all round and some so close."

But at least there was the odd moment of celebration. On 3 September 1940, a Messerschmitt fighter was shot down and managed to crash land, still in pretty good shape, inside the Windsor estate. In early October it was put on display

George, Duke of Kent, whose death in 1942 brought personal tragedy to the royal family

discomfiting, this did lead to the staging of elegant tea parties for the officers.

War at home
None of this did much to disguise the fact that Europe had descended into chaos. One tell-tale sign was the regular arrival of exiled monarchs on British royal doorsteps. King Haakon of Norway and the formidable Dutch monarch Wilhelmina were the first to come a'calling in the spring of 1940 (they both found their own suitably plush digs quite quickly) and they were joined, in the following year, by the dashing young Peter II of Yugoslavia. Having escaped his country only just after coming of age, he was very much taken under the wing of his godfather, George VI, who arranged for Peter to complete his education at Cambridge and smoothed his entry into the RAF.

Elizabeth dons the uniform of her regiment, the Grenadier Guards

and Elizabeth was allowed to clamber into the pilot's seat. All proceeds from the viewings were donated, appropriately enough, to the Royal Borough of Windsor's Spitfire Fund. Not that such jollity could ever obscure the spectre of personal tragedy. It arose, with full force, in August 1942 when an aircraft carrying the king's brother, Prince George, Duke of Kent, crashed into a hillside close to Dunbeath, Scotland. Mystery has always surrounded the flight. Was it really headed, as claimed, to Iceland or to some surreptitious meeting in Sweden? But two facts are irrefutable. George was the first major royal to die on active service for almost 500 years and his family were devastated. Elizabeth felt the loss of her favourite uncle particularly deeply.

Doing one's bit

Perhaps the best medicine was to devote even more time to duties on the home front. As we have seen, Elizabeth had already made an excellent start with the Children's Hour broadcast and was soon helping the Dig for Victory campaign in the cobbled together allotments at Windsor. The princess was always pleased to be called over to her father's desk to have some piece of information from the official Red Boxes explained to her - moments that the king, with the future in mind, took very seriously. Minor public roles were taken on - presidency of the RSPCC and of the Queen Elizabeth Hospital for Children in Bethnal Green and, with the arrival of Elizabeth's 16th birthday in April 1942, a real watershed moment was reached.

She had already been appointed as a colonel of the Grenadier Guards in February, but the red letter day had to wait until April. On the 20th, Elizabeth was presented with a brooch in the shape of the regimental badge, and on the 21st - the princess's birthday - she inspected the troops in Windsor's forecourt. Both the king and queen were in attendance, but Elizabeth took the lead: it was the future monarch's first official public engagement. Before too long, Elizabeth would be observing the Guards during tank manoeuvres at Andover, but 21 April 1942 ended in more relaxed fashion: a vaudeville party with the comedian Tommy Handley topping the bill.

It is a singular princess who turns up at the local labour exchange demanding to be put on

> ## "ELIZABETH'S MOST CELEBRATED CONTRIBUTION TO THE WAR EFFORT WAS JUST AROUND THE CORNER"

the books and, though nothing was ever likely to come of this, Elizabeth eagerly snapped up new opportunities: becoming a Sea Ranger with the rank of bosun, and accompanying her parents on more and more official visits - whether to open homes for sailors in Aberdeen, to explore the shipyards at Sunderland, or inspect the 15 and 622 Lancaster squadrons at RAF Mildenhall. Finally, in 1944, Elizabeth achieved a position of genuine political influence, being appointed as one of the five counsellors of state, the group that formally stood in for the king in the instances that he was indisposed or overseas.

Not all of the plans were a roaring success. The British government was keen to bolster support in Wales - where the nationalist movement was doing good business, especially in the north - and it was proposed that Elizabeth might be recruited in some glorified PR capacity. Perhaps she could be

appointed as constable of Caernarfon Castle or as patron of the Welsh Youth League. The king feared this might be too much of a burden and he was dead set against any association with the League, two of whose leaders were conscientious objectors. These, though, were minor set-backs and Elizabeth's most celebrated contribution to the war effort - one which involved the literal dirtying of hands - was just around the corner.

To the toolboxes...

The Auxiliary Territorial Service (ATS) was established in 1938 as a female branch of the army. It was joined, in the following year, by a rejigged Women's Royal Navy Service and Women's Auxiliary Air Force. The ATS was granted equal status with the male army in 1942, although this was more a matter of discipline - members could

Elizabeth learning the tricks of the trade during her spell as an honorary subaltern in the ATS

The royal family delight the crowds with a VE Day appearance on the Palace balcony

"IN 1942, CONSCRIPTION OF ALL SINGLE WOMEN BETWEEN THE AGES OF 20 AND 30 WAS ENFORCED"

now be court-martialed for desertion – than a giant leap towards gender equality. Women's paypackets remained one-third lighter than those of their male counterparts.

At first, just five major roles were assigned to the service: clerical duty, work as cooks, as storekeepers, drivers and orderlies. This quickly changed as the male contingent of the army was drawn to the battlefield. Women took on a staggering array of responsibilities and trained for their chosen specialism after a few weeks' basic training. The need was such that, in 1942, conscription of all single women between the ages of 20 and 30 was enforced. This was gradually expanded during the war, though women were given the option of factory work or helping to feed the nation as members of the Women's Land Army rather than joining the ATS or its sister services. The numbers involved were impressive. By 1945 the ATS

had 199,000 members and, across the three main services, 640,000 had served at some point during the conflict.

The king was not overly keen on Elizabeth joining up but he knew the war was entering its final stages and that the princess was very unlikely to come in harm's way. She was appointed as an honorary second subaltern in February 1945 and passed out, within a few months, as an honorary junior commander. Elizabeth's presence was, in part, an exercise in boosting morale but she took the training very seriously and, by all accounts, deserved recognition for her aptitude in driving and mechanics. It really was the princess changing tires and spark plugs in all the photos and she really was qualified to manoeuvre vehicles weighing up to three tons.

Admittedly, not every recruit was chauffeur-driven between work and Windsor Castle every morning and evening, or whisked away for lunch in the officers' mess. But Elizabeth's contemporaries

A happier wartime memory: the 1944 wedding of Peter II and Alexandra of Yugoslavia, with George VI serving as best man

remembered a convivial young woman who overcame her bashfulness to enjoy a chat during tea-breaks. It was a meaningful achievement that Elizabeth always remembered fondly.

And then to the balcony

Not that the princess had much time to put her new skills to the test. By May, the whole show was

The VE Day carousing gets underway in central London

Princess Elizabeth in the uniform of the Sea Rangers

over and, on the 8th, Britain prepared to celebrate VE Day. Steps were taken to ensure that central London had adequate supplies of beer and after the solemnities of church services, the mood became increasingly frenzied. Churchill gave one of his predictably rousing speeches at 3pm – "the evil-doers now lie prostate before us" – and the royal family began making regular appearances on the pock-marked balcony at Buckingham Palace, with Elizabeth loyally kitted out in her ATS uniform. The street parties soon kicked off and occasionally got out of hand – erecting a bonfire in the middle of Oxford Street was seen as an exuberance too far by the fire services who, accompanied by boos from street revellers, quickly extinguished the blaze.

The pandemonium, outside a few square miles in London's West End, can easily be exaggerated. As one data-collating agency revealed, most Brits put up the bunting then spent the day "either at home, at small parties, at indoor dances, or in public houses or collected in small groups around the bonfires". A little extra oomph was sometimes added. At Stoke Lacy, in the wilds of Herefordshire, an effigy of Hitler was cast into the flames.

Events in the capital did count, however. Perhaps one-third of the population tuned their radios to 'Bells and Victory Celebrations from London' at 3.30pm and, later in the day, they were back to their radio sets to listen to the king's much-anticipated speech. It's also hard to imagine that they would not have relished the sight of St Paul's and the National Gallery being floodlit for the first time in six years under skies that were finally safe.

That evening, George VI even granted his daughters' unusual request to leave the confines of the palace and mingle with the crowds. "Poor Darlings," he would write in his diary, "they have never had any fun yet," so where was the harm? Margaret, Elizabeth and a small entourage spent a few anonymous hours dancing in the streets – though they were terrified of being recognised by the people – and returned home, safe and sound, at midnight or thereabouts. By this time, as many as 50,000 people had managed to squeeze into Piccadilly Circus.

Over the next few days, glimmers of normality began to appear. For one thing, full weather forecasts returned to newspapers and the radio schedule – during the war, the Met Office had not been willing to make such useful information easily available to the enemy. Less happily, the grief of wartime loss would linger and the austerity would cling on for more years than the revellers on VE Day might have anticipated. Still, for the crowds, a couple of carefree princesses included, 8 May 1945 had been a rather spectacular occasion.

MAKING DO, WINDSOR-STYLE

Like everyone else in Britain, the royal family had to endure the annoyances of rationing

It has always been a little hard to believe the historian AJP Taylor's story of King George VI tucking into a portion of spam served up on a golden plate. The royals did try to play by the rules and the deprivations were about more than appearing to muck in.

Home-grown vegetables were all the rage at Windsor, and perhaps it really was a case of boiled plums for pudding every evening. But owning vast estates came in very handy when it came to supplementing diets. As one servant at Balmoral put it, we ate so much venison it was "a wonder we didn't grow antlers".

Clothes rationing applied as well, though while most Britons had to get by on 66 coupons per year (which had fallen to 41 by 1945), senior royals were granted an additional 1,277 annual coupons each. The president of the Board of Trade, Oliver Lyttelton, announced in 1941 that "we must learn as civilians to be seen in clothes that are not so smart", but this clearly wouldn't do if you were a monarch or princess attending a state function. The royals also benefited from the queen's astute stockpiling of fabric during the pre-war years and the back-catalogue of gleaming outfits in the royal wardrobes was also a boon. Fortunately, Elizabeth was not clothes-crazy and came over very well in knitted jumpers, plaid skirts and simple floral tea dresses. She did provoke one minor fashion trend, however. Her appearances in various military getups did wonders for the sales of peaked caps.

Princess Elizabeth, all understated elegance, on her 18th birthday in 1944

THE WINDSORS AT WAR

George's wartime service is celebrated to this day, but how did his family play their part?

1. MARY, PRINCESS ROYAL
1897-1965

Princess Mary, the king's only sister, became chief controller and later commandant of the Auxiliary Territorial Service (the ATS, to be renamed the Women's Royal Army Corps after the war). She visited units of the ATS as well as various wartime canteens and welfare organisations.

2. ALICE, DUCHESS OF GLOUCESTER
1901-2004

Alice worked with both the Red Cross as well as the Order of St John. She was the Queen's Deputy as commandant-in-chief of the Nursing Corps. When war began, she was appointed head of the Women's Auxiliary Air Force (the WAAF), becoming its director and air chief commandant in 1943.

3. HENRY, DUKE OF GLOUCESTER
1900-74

The king's younger brother, Prince Henry had pursued a career in the British Army and was made a major general in 1937. When the war began, he was appointed chief liaison officer to the British Expeditionary Force sent to France. A proposal made in the House of Commons in 1942 that he be made commander in chief of the Army was quickly squashed.

4. PRINCESS MARGARET
1930-2002

Though too young to join the ATS, Princess Margaret often appeared in various morale-boosting press photographs, like tending the allotment she shared with her sister and learning how to operate a stirrup pump in order to put out fires caused by bombing. She appeared often in family photographs.

5. PRINCESS ELIZABETH
1926-2022

The current British monarch made a very popular wartime BBC Radio broadcast in 1940 on 'Children's Hour', and was often pictured in the press. In 1945 she became a Second Lieutenant in the ATS where she learned how to drive and service army trucks, becoming especially knowledgeable on the subject of sparking plugs.

6. QUEEN ELIZABETH
1900-2002

The king's consort's main role during the war was to support her husband in his many wartime activities, especially visiting bombed areas and generally showing that the monarchy was as involved as ordinary people in the struggle for victory. Her sunny personality was a powerful factor in maintaining high national morale.

7. GEORGE, DUKE OF KENT
1902-42

The king's youngest surviving brother, Prince George was appointed an Air Vice Marshal in the Royal Air Force when the war broke out. George was an effective public speaker, and even went to the United States in 1941 where, for example, he personally addressed aircraft workers in Baltimore, Maryland. In 1942 he was killed on a tour of duty when the plane carrying him crashed in the Scottish Highlands.

8. MARINA, DUCHESS OF KENT
1906-68

Widowed in 1942, the duchess continued to play an active role in promoting the Red Cross and the First Aid Service. One photograph from 1943 shows her joining a forces sing-song at the United Nations Forces' Club in London.

© Getty

9. WALLIS, DUCHESS OF WINDSOR
1896-1986

Thought to have been far too sympathetic towards the Nazi regime before the Second World War began, Wallis, Duchess of Windsor, loyally played her part by helping her husband carry out his official royal duties abroad in the Bahamas.

10. EDWARD, DUKE OF WINDSOR
1894-1972

Despite his ill-judged visit to Nazi Germany in 1937, where he was photographed with the duchess being warmly welcomed by a beaming Adolf Hitler, the former king wished to serve his country once the Second World War broke out. After spending a largely unprofitable time in Madrid, Spain, he was eventually made governor-general of the British colony of the Bahamas in 1940, where he served until 1945.

LOVE

THE PRINCE, THE NAZIS AND THE BROKEN HOME

Discover how the Queen's "liege man of life and limb" overcame a tragic upbringing and emerged as a war hero and prince consort

P rince Philip, Duke of Edinburgh, was one of the most recognisable men in the world. As the husband of Queen Elizabeth II, he represented the British monarchy for over 70 years and is the longest-serving consort of a reigning British monarch. Along with the Queen, he did much to represent the royal family as an unchanging institution in a world that has changed almost beyond recognition since Elizabeth succeeded to the throne in 1952. However, on Philip's part this security was in deep contrast to his early life, which was formed by war, neglect, tragedy and endurance. In many ways his long, successful marriage and subsequent family compensated for the trials of his youth.

Philip was born on 10 June 1921 on the Greek island of Corfu at Mons Repos, the only son of Prince Andrew of Greece and Denmark and Princess Alice of Battenberg, who already had four daughters: Cecilie, Sophie, Margarita and Theodora. Although typically seen as British today, Philip was born as Prince of Greece and Denmark. This dual title was reflected in his name. He was

christened 'Philippos' but he belonged to the Danish-German House of Schleswig-Holstein-Sonderburg-Glücksburg. To add to the confusion, Philip was not a British subject at birth but did have family ties to England. His maternal grandfather, Prince Louis of Battenberg, was a naturalised British citizen who had adopted the surname of 'Mountbatten' during World War I. Philip was related to the British royal family through Queen Victoria, but he was also sixth in line to the Greek throne and his paternal uncle Constantine I was the ruling king. Nevertheless, his wider European connections would soon come in very handy for Philip as he was born during a turbulent time for Greece, and his stay in the country of his birth would not last long.

Philip's father was absent at his birth as he was away fighting in the Greek army during the Greco-Turkish War (1919-22). During this conflict, Andrew was the commander of the Greek Second Army Corps, but he proved to be an ineffectual general. At the pivotal Battle of Sakarya on 19 September 1921, he refused to obey the orders of his superior officer and tried to work to his

own battle plan. Unfortunately this lack of co-ordination and communication contributed to a battlefield stalemate, and subsequently the war was lost. Andrew was relieved of his command and a year later he was arrested as part of the 11 September 1922 Revolution. This was a revolt of the Greek armed forces against the government, who they held responsible for the Turkish victory. It led to the downfall of the Greek monarchy and the abdication of King Constantine. As the brother of Constantine and a disgraced army commander, Andrew was in deep trouble. He was accused of treason and initially sentenced to death. General Pangalos, the Greek minister of war, asked him, "How many children have you?" When Andrew replied, Pangalos reportedly said, "Poor things, what a pity they will soon be orphans."

When Princess Alice heard of Andrew's plight, she travelled to Athens to plead for his life but she was not permitted to see her husband, so she turned to her British relatives for help. King George V, who was possibly haunted by not allowing his cousin Tsar Nicholas

Philip (second on the left) started his education at the MacJannet American School in Saint-Cloud, France

"HE WAS A GREEK PRINCE LIVING IN FRANCE BEING EDUCATED IN A BRITISH FASHION"

II of Russia and his family to seek asylum in Britain during World War I, urged for a British intervention to evacuate the family.

A Greek court banished Andrew from Greece for life and he was released in December 1922. He was lucky: six other senior members of the government were tried and executed. Soon afterwards a Royal Navy gunboat, HMS Calypso, evacuated the family from Corfu. Prince Philip, who was still a baby, was reputedly carried out to the ship in a makeshift cot made out of an orange box. For the infant, it was the start of decades of stateless wandering. From the moment Philip left Corfu on 3 December 1922 until he moved into

Clarence House as Princess Elizabeth's husband in the late 1940s, he had no permanent home.

The family tried to settle in France at Saint-Cloud near Paris, where Andrew and Alice borrowed a house. From the start they lived in relative poverty. Alice was able to keep the family together on a limited allowance from her brother and Andrew was able to contribute a small legacy that he had inherited, but they mostly relied on borrowed funds and hand-me-downs.

Relatives paid the children's school fees, with Philip's early education at the MacJannet American School in Paris. His life was confused – he was a Greek prince living in France but being educated in a British fashion. His stateless identity meant that he could formulate his own, which he

later explained, "If anything I've thought of myself as Scandinavian, particularly Danish. We spoke English at home. The others learned Greek. I could understand a certain amount of it. But then the conversation would go into French. Then it went into German, because we had German cousins. If you couldn't think of a word in one language, you tended to go off in another."

In 1928, Philip went to Britain for the first time to attend Cheam School. He appears to have been a somewhat boisterous child who needed some discipline. Alice wrote to the school in 1929 asking his tutors to form a Cub Scouts company for her son with a hint of anxiety: "The training would have such an excellent influence on him... I should be infinitely grateful if you could manage it as soon as possible."

By this stage, Philip's family life was already beginning to collapse. Alice, who had been born deaf, was on the verge of a nervous breakdown. There has been much speculation as to what caused this. It has been variously attributed to the ordeal of the family's exile from Greece, the regular separations from her children as they attended different schools, a traumatic menopause, manic depression and even a possible religious crisis. It may have been one or a combination of these factors, but for whatever reason, Philip's mother was placed in a Swiss sanatorium in 1931.

At around the same time, Philip's sisters all married within nine months of each other between 1930-31 and moved away to settle in Germany. Prince Andrew, who had spent more and more time away from the Parisian family home, finally left altogether and moved to the south of France with a mistress. One relation said he was "a deeply unhappy man". Philip's sister Sophie said, "We all sort of disappeared and the house in Saint-Cloud was closed down." His parents had effectively relinquished responsibility for their son. This does not mean that they did not care for him - indeed, by all accounts he was much loved - but the circumstances of their own lives meant that they were unable to look after him properly. He was just ten years old and would receive no word from his mother between 1932 and 1937. When Philip was asked about this time years later, his reply was stoic and pragmatic: "It's simply what happened. The family broke up. My mother was ill, my sisters were married, my father was in the south of France. I just had to get on with it. You do. One does."

In the aftermath of this disintegration, the British part of Philip's family took a large part of responsibility for his care. His maternal grandmother, Princess Victoria, sent him to live with his uncle George, Marquis of Milford Haven.

He was Philip's guardian for the next seven years and became a surrogate father. Philip would become close friends with George's son David, who later was best man at his wedding to Princess Elizabeth. The two boys attended Cheam School, where Philip excelled at sport. The marquis would often come to watch him and his son play in school matches. The Milford Havens gave Philip a sense of stability that was lacking elsewhere, but he remembered the upheaval as confusing. When he was later asked what language was spoken at home he replied, "What do you mean, at home?"

In 1933 Philip's second sister Theodora reappeared in his life and set him down the path towards a different education by introducing him to a significant mentor: Kurt Hahn. Theodora had married Berthold, Margrave of Baden, whose father had been Imperial Germany's last chancellor. Hahn had been the chancellor's personal secretary and knew the family, but he was also a committed educationalist. He was Jewish and a German patriot who had been involved in the 1919 Treaty of Versailles. He had been so upset at the Allied treatment of post-

This portrait of Philip's mother, Princess Alice of Battenberg, was painted in 1907. Alice was deaf but could lip-read in several languages

THE GRECO-TURKISH WAR (1919-22)

Prince Philip's early life was largely influenced by a disastrous conflict between Greece and Turkey in the aftermath of World War I

When the Ottoman Empire collapsed at the end of World War I, Greece moved troops into western Turkey to protect the large Greek population and to assert its historical claim over the region. The Greeks and Turks had long been traditional enemies, and the Greek invasion was largely informed by a nationalist dream to create a greater Greece based on the Byzantine Empire, with Constantinople (now Istanbul) as its seat of government.

On 15 May 1919, Greek troops landed at Smyrna and occupied the city under the cover of the Allied navies. They already occupied Eastern Thrace and went on to create a Greek zone of occupation that covered most of western Asia Minor. At this stage, King Constantine took command of the army.

The western allies formally partitioned Turkey at the 1920 Treaty of Sèvres, giving Greece Smyrna and Eastern Thrace as a reward for their contribution in World War I. The local Greek Christian population welcomed the invaders as liberators, but the Muslim Turks saw them as occupiers. Turkish revolutionary leader Mustafa Kemal rejected Sèvres and launched a national war against the Greeks. He halted the Greek advance at the First and Second Battles of Inonu in

early 1921 and the tide began to turn. And while the British refused to militarily assist the Greeks, the Turks received substantial help from the USSR.

The advancing Greeks met fierce resistance at the Battle of Sakarya, which was fought over 21 days between August and September 1921. Both sides became exhausted and contemplated withdrawal but the Greeks withdrew first. This near-stalemate definitively turned the course of the war and the Greeks advanced no further as they were hampered by a poor economy and a lack of strategic and operational planning.

An armistice was signed after a decisive Turkish victory at Dumlupinar in August 1922, and the Greeks left Turkey. The resulting Treaty of Lausanne saw an exchange of populations between the two countries; 500,000 Turks left Greece, but almost all of the 1.5 million Greeks living in Turkish Anatolia and Thrace were expelled. Greece had huge problems trying to cater for them in a ruined economy, becoming internationally isolated and internally divided. The monarchy, largely blamed for the defeat, was abolished and the war later became known as the Asia Minor Catastrophe.

A FAMILY DIVIDED Find out what became of Prince Philip's broken family

© Mary Evans

5. PRINCESS ALICE
1885-1969
Philip's mother, Princess Alice of Battenberg, was committed to several sanitariums in the 1920s and 1930s. Upon her release, she found solace in religion and became a nun. She died in 1969 at Buckingham Palace.

6. PRINCE ANDREW
1882-1944
Having left his family, Prince Andrew took up residence with his mistress on a yacht in the French Riviera. At the funeral of Cecilie in 1937, he met his wife for the first time in six years. In 1944 he died of heart failure in Monte Carlo.

1. THEODORA
1906-69
Second-born to Prince Andrew of Greece and Denmark and Princess Alice of Battenberg, Theodora married Berthold, Margrave of Baden. She died in 1969, outliving her husband, but outlived by her mother.

2. CECILIE
1911-37
Tragically dying in a plane crash at the age of 26, Cecilie married Georg Donatus. Cecilie died with her husband, two sons and unborn baby, but left behind a daughter, Joanna. Two years later, Joanna died of meningitis.

3. SOPHIE
1914-2001
Sophie was first to marry. In 1930 she wed Prince Christoph of Hesse. He died 13 years later. She later married Prince George William of Hanover. Sophie was godmother to Prince Edward, Philip's fourth child.

4. MARGARITA
1905-81
The eldest sister of the family, Margarita married Prince Gottfried of Hohenlohe-Langenburg. They had six children together. Dying at the age of 76, she outlived her husband by 21 years.

war Germany that he helped to coin the term 'Kriegsschuldluge' ('the lie of war guilt'). Ironically, the deeply anti-Semitic Nazi Party would use this as a slogan for revenge and rearmament.

In 1920, he and the Baden family founded a school at Schloss Salem in Baden-Württemberg,

© Getty

Philip c.1935 at Gordonstoun dressed in costume for a school production of *Macbeth*

and it was here that Theodora sent Philip in autumn 1933. It was an anxious time to move to Germany as Adolf Hitler had recently come to power. He had only been in office for a few months, but it was enough to create political tensions, with Hahn himself being arrested for protesting against the Nazis. For Philip the move was bad timing and his brother-in-law admitted, "He wasn't really integrated into the community. He had little opportunity to make real friends, and he spoke very little German. He was really very isolated." In a sinister twist, the Nazis promoted the Hitler Youth Movement in the school, where participants would use the Nazi salute. Philip apparently laughed at this, as the salute was the same gesture that the boys at Schloss Salem used to indicate that they wanted to go to the toilet.

By 1934 Philip was sent back to Britain and was sent to a new school in Scotland that had been established by the now-exiled Hahn: Gordonstoun. The teaching methods developed by Hahn

were radical and innovative. He believed that adolescents should be respected but were also susceptible to the corruptions of society. Hahn postulated that there were was a six-fold decay of civilisation, which he called 'The Six Declines of Modern Youth'. They were the decline of: fitness, initiative and enterprise, memory and imagination, skill and care, self-discipline, and compassion. Gordonstoun pupils were taught to counter them. For instance, they rose at 7am each day, donned shorts and ran barefoot for 300 yards to the washroom where they showered in cold water both in winter and summer.

Philip was hardy, energetic and competitive, and flourished under this apparently tough regime. He excelled at hockey and sailing, and in his last year became head boy. Hahn's philosophy had a great impact on Philip and many years later he called on him to help found the Duke of Edinburgh's Award programme. Today the award scheme is active in 144 countries and recognises young

Painted by Hungarian artist Philip de László in 1913, Prince Andrew of Greece and Denmark was a prominent commander of the Greek army, but was exiled for life

Philip's elder sister Cecilie was a member of the Nazi party

Philip's marriage to Princess Elizabeth in November 1947 gave him a domestic stability that he had never known

"HE WAS JUST TEN YEARS OLD AND WOULD RECEIVE NO WORD FROM HIS MOTHER"

people's achievements in self-improvement based on Hahn's Six Declines of Modern Youth. Such was Hahn's influence that when he died in 1974, Philip read the story of the Good Samaritan at his memorial service.

Despite Philip's achievements at Gordonstoun, he could not escape the fact that he was still very isolated. In the five years that he attended the school, neither George Milford Haven nor Philip's other British guardian, Lord Louis Mountbatten, visited him. This is an extraordinary lapse for men who were technically responsible for him. During term-time there were long discussions about where Philip would go for his holidays.

Then, towards the end of his time at Gordonstoun, Philip was hit by a family tragedy. On 19 November 1937, his pregnant sister Cecilie was killed in plane crash in Belgium, along with her husband, two children and unborn child. She had been flying to England to attend a wedding. Hahn conveyed the news to Philip, but the 16-year-

old did not break down, which led his headmaster to recall, "His sorrow was that of a man." Nor did his fellow pupils remember Philip showing any signs of grief, with one remembering, "I suppose he just buried his feelings."

Philip travelled alone to attend the funerals in Germany. It was a tragically strange occasion. Nazi officials surrounded the funeral parties, but it was also the first time that Philip's parents had seen each other and their surviving children for years. They were the worst circumstances for a reunion, but afterwards, Philip returned to Britain to fend for himself again.

The next year, 1938, brought new purpose to Philip's life in more ways than one. Under the

advice of his father and Lord Mountbatten, he decided to join the Royal Navy and enrolled at the Britannia Royal Naval College at Dartmouth. He excelled at training and almost passed with top marks. His contemporary, Terence Lewin, who later became First Sea Lord, said, "Prince Philip was a highly talented seaman. No doubt about it. If he hadn't become what he did, he would have been First Sea Lord and not me."

This was an intense time to join the Navy as Britain was on the brink of war with Germany, but Philip's time at Dartmouth coincided with the first meeting of his future wife. In July 1939, Philip was put in charge

THE SISTERS WHO MARRIED NAZIS

Some of Philip's siblings had sinister connections to the Third Reich

One sign of Philip's highly divided family was that some of his sisters had connections to the Nazi Party. All four had married into the German nobility: Margarita had married Gottfried, Prince of Hohenlohe-Langenburg; Theodora married Berthold, Margrave of Baden; Cecilie married Georg Donatus, Grand Duke of Hesse; and Sophie married Prince Christoph of Hesse. It was traditional for European royal families to marry into foreign noble houses, but in the context of the 1930s, it was an out-of-date practice, particularly in the wake of World War I. Many surviving nobles tried to protect their positions by aligning with the radical social changes that were occurring throughout Europe. In the case of Germany, some sought to curry favour with the Nazis.

Sophie's husband, Prince Christoph, and his brother Philipp were great-grandsons of Queen Victoria and enthusiastic Nazis. Christoph was a prominent SS colonel who was attached to Himmler's personal staff and was the head of the intelligence service, the 'Forschungsamt', which spied on Nazi opponents under the command of Hermann Goering.

Philipp had joined the Nazis in 1930 and was their governor in Hesse in 1933, later serving as a liaison between Hitler and Mussolini. Sophie and Christoph even named their eldest son Karl Adolf in Hitler's honour, and Sophie said that Hitler was a "charming and seemingly modest man".

On 1 May 1937, Cecilie and her husband, Georg, Duke of Hesse, also joined the Nazi Party, but they were killed in a plane crash. Their funerals became a Nazi pageant. Prince Philip walked alongside Prince Christoph, who wore his SS uniform, while Philipp wore the brown shirt of the SA. There were also uniformed soldiers, and many onlookers gave the Hitler salute. Goering attended and there were messages of condolences from Hitler and Goebbels.

When Prince Philip married Princess Elizabeth ten years later, the British royal family excluded his surviving sisters and their husbands from attending the wedding. It was largely out of embarrassment, but it also took into consideration the anti-German feeling in Britain when the horrors of the Nazi regime had been realised.

During World War II, Philip was first officer on board HMS Whelp

Prince Philipp of Hesse was a member of the Nazi Party and the brother-in-law of Princess Sophie, Philip's sister

of entertaining his distant cousins, 13-year-old Princess Elizabeth and her younger sister Margaret when they visited the college. They had met in 1934 and in 1937 at George VI's coronation, but on this occasion Elizabeth fell for Philip. Over the next few years they would write letters to each other, but for the moment there were other priorities. There was a war to be fought.

Philip's war service began when he was posted to HMS Ramillies in Ceylon in January 1940. In the war's early days, he was posted far from action as Greece was not at war, and the British did not want a Greek prince to be killed on a Royal Navy ship. However, this changed when Italy invaded Greece and Philip became an active participant.

At the Battle of Cape Matapan off the Greek coast in March 1941, Philip served as a midshipman on HMS Valiant where he was in charge of operating the ship's searchlight to pick out ships during the night. He recalled: "I reported that I had a target in sight and was ordered to 'open shutter'. The beam lit up a stationary cruiser and at this point all hell broke loose, as all our eight 15-inch guns, plus those of the flagship, plus HMS Barham's, started firing at the stationary cruiser, which disappeared in an explosion and a cloud of smoke. I was then ordered to 'train left' and lit up another Italian cruiser, which was given the same treatment." The ships identified by Philip were two of five Italian warships that were

Philip works in his office upon returning from service

"DURING TERM-TIME THERE WERE LONG DISCUSSIONS ABOUT WHERE PHILIP WOULD GO FOR HIS HOLIDAYS"

sunk by the British with the loss of 2,300 sailors. It was Italy's greatest naval defeat and Philip was mentioned in dispatches for his courage and awarded the Greek Cross of Valour.

The next year, at the age of 21, Philip was promoted to become one of the youngest first lieutenants in the Navy, and in July 1943 he was once again in action, this time aboard HMS Wallace taking part in the Allied invasion of Sicily. During a night attack, Wallace came under bombardment from a German plane. One yeoman sailor aboard the ship, Harry Hargreaves, recalled in a 2003 interview: "It was obvious that we were a target and they would not stop until we had suffered a fatal hit. It was like being blindfolded and trying to evade an enemy whose only problem was getting his aim right. There was no doubt in anyone's mind that a direct hit was inevitable."

During a lull in the attack Philip acted quickly. "The first lieutenant [Philip] went into hurried conversation with the captain, and the next thing a wooden raft was being put together on deck." This raft was attached with smoke floats that

created the illusion of debris ablaze on the water. The German plane was fooled into attacking the raft and the ship slipped away under the cover of darkness. Hargreaves praised Philip's initiative: "It had been marvellously quick thinking. Prince Philip saved our lives that night. I suppose there would have been a few survivors, but certainly the ship would have been sunk. He was always very courageous and resourceful." Philip himself later talked about his plan in a BBC interview, describing it as "a frightfully good wheeze... we got away with it". Despite his nonchalance, even he conceded, "It was a very unpleasant sensation."

Philip ended his war aboard HMS Whelp, which was one of the ships that took part in the formal surrender of Japanese forces on 2 September 1945. He recalled, "Being in Tokyo Bay with the surrender ceremony taking place in the battle ship, which was what, 200 yards away and you could see what was going on with a pair of binoculars, it was a great relief." After the surrender, his ship took on former prisoners of war and he was shocked by their appearance. "These people were

naval people. They were emaciated... tears pouring down their cheeks, they just drank their tea, they couldn't really speak. It was a most extraordinary sensation."

Now that the war was over he expected to continue in his naval career, but fate had determined a different future for him.

The Battle of Cape Matapan, during which Philip was in charge of operating the ship's searchlight

THE WEDDING OF PRINCESS ELIZABETH & PRINCE PHILIP

As Britain recovered from the horrors of World War II, it basked in the romantic love story of Princess Elizabeth and Prince Philip

Over the last seven decades, Queen Elizabeth and Prince Philip have been the foundation of the British monarchy. The story of their relationship, from a young romance to their marriage, endeared them to the public at a time when the majority of royals married for duty rather than for love. Their wedding came at a time when the people of Britain, weary from the war, craved a distraction, becoming one of the most celebrated events of the 20th century.

Princess Elizabeth was just eight years old when she first set eyes on her third cousin, Prince Philip, at the wedding of Princess Marina of Greece and Denmark to Prince George, Duke of Kent, in 1934. Five years later they would meet again, at the Royal Naval College in Dartmouth in July 1939. This time Elizabeth, now 13 years old, fell head over heels in love for Philip, who had turned into a handsome 18-year-old man.

The pair managed to spend a lot of time together that day, as Philip's uncle, Lord Louis Mountbatten, had arranged for his nephew to chaperone both Elizabeth and her sister, Margaret. After connecting at the college, Elizabeth and Philip agreed to exchange letters while they were apart and soon enough, the princess started to keep a framed photo of her beloved by her bed.

With the outbreak of World War II just months later, the couple were separated over the next six years, just like millions of others across the country. While Philip served in the British Royal Navy, the princess trained as a driver and mechanic, working for the Auxiliary Territorial Service in 1945. They remained in contact during such harrowing times, with the latter even making a brief visit to Windsor to watch the princess perform in a pantomime with her sister.

When the war finally ended in 1945, there was a sigh of relief across Great Britain. Elizabeth and Philip were still in love and it became obvious to onlookers that their romance was indeed serious. Elizabeth's father, King George VI, invited Philip to Balmoral in 1946. It was during this visit that the prince took the plunge and asked Elizabeth to marry him, after seeking permission from her father. George consented, but on the condition that the engagement remain a secret until Elizabeth's 21st birthday in April 1947.

However, this was not just about giving Elizabeth time to consider her decision. Her father, along with the rest of the royal family, were concerned that Philip was not a suitable choice for the husband of the future queen. There were no advantages to be made from a marriage between the two - although Philip was a prince, he was practically penniless, and his family had been exiled from Greece after the abdication of his uncle, King Constantine I.

In addition to this, Elizabeth's family were well aware of the chaotic situation of Philip's parents. While Elizabeth had a close and loving upbringing, Philip was left alone to be raised in boarding schools. His mother, Princess Alice of Battenberg, was suffering with severe mental illness, while his philandering father had abandoned the family. With parents such as these, there were grave doubts about Philip's ability to remain faithful to Elizabeth.

There were also concerns about Philip's connection to the Nazis in the wake of World War II. All four of his older sisters had married Nazis and when one of them, Cecile, died in a plane crash in 1937, a young Philip was pictured at her funeral surrounded by the Nazis.

The young couple looked very much in love on their wedding day

Elizabeth walking up the aisle at Westminster Abbey with her father

Of course, it was also impossible to forget the domineering presence of Philip's uncle and mentor, Lord Mountbatten. Ambitious and determined, it was no secret that Mountbatten was actively campaigning in favour of the relationship - to the point where Philip apparently admitted that his uncle was placing a lot of pressure on him to ask for Elizabeth's hand in marriage.

It is said that Elizabeth's mother, Queen Elizabeth, referred to her future son-in-law as "the Hun" and that even the prime minister, Winston Churchill, was suspicious of the prince. Though Elizabeth was excited about her future with Philip, her family secretly hoped that within a year she would have changed her mind.

Elizabeth may have been a naturally shy woman, but her family wholly underestimated her determination to marry Philip. Adamant that she would only marry him, King George and Queen Elizabeth were eventually forced to accept their daughter's relationship. In the lead up to the announcement of their engagement, Prince Philip

"WEDDING FEVER WAS RUNNING HIGH THROUGHOUT THE NATION"

renounced his Greek and Danish titles, and he became a naturalised British citizen, subsequently adopting the last name 'Mountbatten', which was from his mother's British family. Philip also converted to Anglicanism in preparation for his marriage to the future supreme governor of the Church of England.

On 9 July 1947, less than three months after Elizabeth's 21st birthday, the royal engagement was announced to the world. While the couple basked in the happiness, it seemed that it was not only Elizabeth's family that had reservations about the match. A newspaper poll that was held soon after the announcement indicated that 40 per cent of the public were against the marriage - unsurprising, as Philip was considered too 'German' following the conclusion of the war.

Yet when it became clear that the couple were marrying for love rather than duty, those who

initially opposed the marriage soon warmed up to it. After all, a glamorous royal wedding was a welcome distraction for many in Great Britain and a great way to boost morale in the country.

With the wedding date set for the 20 November and with just four months to plan the event, preparations quickly got under way. It wasn't until mid August that the design for Elizabeth's wedding dress, by Sir Norman Hartnell, was approved, giving the renowned designer less than three months to create his masterpiece.

Wedding fever was running high throughout the nation (and worldwide), but with post-war austerity still in place, Elizabeth had to save up her clothing ration coupons in order to pay for the material of her dress - in total, it took 3,000 coupons. To help her, hundreds of brides-to-be sent their own coupons to the princess so that she could use them. Although this was a very endearing gesture,

© Getty

DRESSING FOR THE DATE

Fit for a queen, Elizabeth's wedding dress was a sumptuous but modest creation perfect for the post-war years

1. PATRIOTIC PATRONAGE

The wedding dress was made with sumptuous duchesse satin, which had been sourced from the firm of Wintherthur, near Dunfermline in Scotland.

2. ART INSPIRATION

Hartnell stated that he had been inspired by Botticelli's famous painting *Primavera*, which symbolises the coming of spring - hence the appliqué motifs of flowers on the bridal train.

3. DAINTY DECORATION

The dress was decorated with crystals and around 10,000 seed pearls, which had been imported from the United States. Meanwhile, the satin for the appliqué was produced at Lullingstone Castle in Kent.

4. DELICATE SHOES

Elizabeth wore ivory duchesse satin high-heeled sandals, which were trimmed with silver and seed peal buckles and made by Edward Rayne.

5. PEARLS FIT FOR A PRINCESS

Elizabeth's double strand pearls, gifted by her father, were actually two separate necklaces. The shorter one is known as the Queen Anne necklace and was said to have belonged to Queen Anne, while the second was known as Queen Caroline, which was said to have belonged to the wife of King George II.

6. ELEGANT DESIGN

The dress had a simple cut with a fitted bodice and a heart-shaped neckline, with a low v-pointed waist and a floor-length panelled skirt.

7. BRIDAL TRAIN

Elizabeth had a 15-foot full court train that attached on the shoulders and was made of silk tulle, embroidered with pearl, crystal and transparent appliqué tulle.

Crowds lined the streets just to get a glimpse of the bride

A ROYAL HONEYMOON

How Elizabeth and Philip spent their first few days as newlyweds

As the bride emerged from Buckingham Palace to embark on her honeymoon, she wore a dress and velvet coat with a bonnet trimmed with ostrich feathers, designed by Norman Hartnell, in an appropriate shade of love-in-the-mist blue. The king and queen, along with Princess Alice, came out to wave the couple off.

Elizabeth and Philip were driven to Waterloo station in an open landau carriage so that the waiting crowds could see them – to ward off the cold, there were hot water bottles of the floor of the carriage, along with Elizabeth's beloved corgi, Susan. As the carriage departed, the newlyweds were showered with rose petals rather than traditional confetti.

Elizabeth and Philip travelled to Broadlands in Hampshire, the home of Philip's uncle Earl Mountbatten, where they spent the first half of their honeymoon in an 18th-century lodge – in 2007, the couple re-created their iconic honeymoon photo at Broadlands. Afterwards, they moved on to Birkhall Lodge, which was part of the Balmoral estate, to see out the rest of their honeymoon.

While they were away, Elizabeth and Philip released a statement expressing the gratitude they felt for all the well-wishes they had received. The princess also kept in touch with her family and lovingly informed her mother that Philip was "an angel".

"PRINCE PHILIP WAS MADE DUKE OF EDINBURGH"

the coupons all had to be returned to their owners as it would have been illegal for Elizabeth to use them because they belonged to others.

The government did provide Elizabeth with 200 extra coupons to pay for her wedding dress while Philip, never one for extravagance and spending, planned to wear his naval uniform for the big day. The couple would marry at London's Westminster Abbey, where Elizabeth's parents had married just over 24 years earlier, making the princess the tenth member of the royal family to be wed in this spectacular setting.

It was decided that the princess would have eight bridesmaids including her sister, Princess Margaret, her cousin Princess Alexandra of Kent, Lady Caroline Montagu-Douglas-Scott, Lady Mary Cambridge, The Hon Pamela Mountbatten, The Hon Margaret Elphinstone, Lady Elizabeth Lambart and Diana Bowes-Lyon.

As for Philip's best man, he chose David Mountbatten,

Marquess of Milford Haven, while Prince William of Gloucester and Prince Michael of Kent would serve as page boys. In total, 2,000 guests were to be invited to the wedding ceremony, many of whom were heads of state, such as Princess Juliana and Prince Bernhard of the Netherlands and the king of Iraq. Notably absent would be Philip's sisters as well as Elizabeth's uncle, the duke of Windsor, who had caused a constitutional crisis just a decade earlier by abdicating the throne.

The king and queen held a grand ball at Buckingham Palace just two days before the wedding to celebrate their daughter's upcoming marriage. The usually reserved King George even led a conga line through all of the state rooms in the palace. On the morning of the wedding, Prince Philip was made duke of Edinburgh, earl of Merioneth and Baron Greenwich. The day before, King George had bestowed the title of 'His Royal Highness' on Philip, which meant that for a few hours, the prince had the unusual title of His Royal Highness Sir Philip Mountbatten.

The beaming bride after her fairytale wedding

Elizabeth and Philip are pictured here after announcing their engagement

Elizabeth in 1939, the same year she fell in love with Philip

The magnificent wedding cake

Philip had spent the night before his wedding at Kensington Palace, and with hordes of photographers outside in the bitter cold waiting for him to emerge, he arranged tea and coffee for them. Meanwhile, Elizabeth was getting ready at Buckingham Palace, even applying her own makeup for the wedding.

Just like any wedding day, not everything went as smoothly as the princess would have liked. Her delicate bridal bouquet, delivered that morning and made of white orchids and a sprig of myrtle, had gone missing. The myrtle had come from Osborne House, where Queen Victoria had planted a cutting that had been given to her by her husband, Prince Albert's, grandmother. As panic set in, it turned out that a footman had placed the bride's bouquet in a cool room to keep it fresh and prevent it from wilting before the ceremony.

The bouquet was not the only unfortunate mishap of the morning. Elizabeth's mother had lent her the Queen Mary Fringe Tiara to be her something borrowed on her special day. As it was being placed on her head, disaster struck as the diamond tiara suddenly snapped. Standing by in case of an emergency was the court jeweller, who was rushed to his workroom by a police escort. Elizabeth waited anxiously and her mother quickly reassured her that the tiara would be fixed in time - and it was.

To top off the issues for the bride-to-be, the necklace that she supposed to wear, a double strand of pearls gifted to her by her parents, had been put on display at St James's Palace. To get them in time, Elizabeth's private secretary raced to the palace, borrowing the car of King Haakon VII of Norway to make it in time.

THE ENGAGEMENT RING

Philip went to great lengths to design a ring fit for a queen

It was no secret that Philip was practically penniless, which was a huge obstacle when it came to creating the engagement ring of Elizabeth's dreams. Aware that her son wanted to propose to his beloved, Princess Alice gave him her tiara, which had been a gift from Tsar Nicholas II and Tsarina Alexandra. It was a sweet gesture, as Alice sacrificed her tiara to help Philip propose to the princess.

With the help of London-based jewellers Philip Antrobus Ltd, Philip used the diamonds from his mother's tiara to create a platinum and diamond engagement ring. The three-carat diamond solitaire is flanked by ten small diamonds, all set in platinum. While making her engagement ring, Philip also used other diamonds to make Elizabeth a beautiful bracelet as a wedding gift. Apparently, the prince wanted to design a ring that Elizabeth could wear with every outfit for every occasion, which was not a usual thing to consider at the time.

However, this was not the only wedding gift that Philip gave to Elizabeth. It is said that on the morning of the wedding, Philip decided to permanently quit smoking. His decision behind this was reportedly out of respect for his soon-to-be wife, who disliked smoking and was concerned about her father's habit, particularly as his health was steadily declining.

Elizabeth is always pictured wearing her beautiful engagement ring

Princess Elizabeth and her father arrive at Westminster Abbey

Despite the bumps along the way, the princess and the prince were finally ready for their wedding, which was due to start at 11.30am. The royal parties arrived at the abbey in large carriage processions, past the thousands of onlookers who had lined the streets to get a glimpse of the royal bride. Queen Elizabeth and Princess Margaret were the first to arrive, followed by Dowager Queen Mary.

Prince Philip left Kensington Palace accompanied by his best man and entered the abbey through a door near Poet's Corner. Meanwhile, Elizabeth made her way inside the decadent Irish State Coach, with her father by her side, escorted by the Household Cavalry. As the coach approached the abbey, the bells of St Margaret's Church rang out to announce the princess's arrival.

Outside, the princess was joined by her large bridal party. As the radiant bride made her way inside Westminster Abbey, she must have been acutely aware that the entire ceremony was being recorded and broadcast by BBC radio to 200 million people. Waiting at the High Altar was the archbishop of Canterbury, Geoffrey Fisher, who officiated the wedding.

At the High Altar there were large vases filled with white lilies, roses, pink carnations, camellia foliage, variegated ivy and chrysanthemums. Clement Attlee, the prime minister at the time, and other politicians were sat in the choir stalls, with King George VI and Queen Elizabeth sat in the south side of the Sanctuary.

The organist and master of the choristers at the abbey, William Neil McKie, was the director for the music. The ceremony began with a fanfare specifically composed for the wedding by Arnold Bax, while McKie also composed a motet for the wedding, "We wait for thy loving kindness, O God." Sir Edward Cuthbert Bairstow sung a rendition of Psalm 67 and in total, there were 91 singers at the wedding with the combined choirs of Westminster

The newlyweds waved to the crowds outside Buckingham Palace

"ELIZABETH'S DRESS WAS EXHIBITED AT ST JAMES'S PALACE BEFORE EMBARKING ON A TOUR"

Abbey, the Chapel Royal and St George's Chapel in Windsor.

The couple exchanged their vows. Elizabeth's wedding ring was made from a nugget of Welsh gold, which came from the Clogau St David's mine, near Dolgellau. The gold had been given as a gift to Queen Elizabeth to make her wedding ring and, eventually, the those of Princess Margaret, Princess Anne and Princess Diana were all made with it.

After the couple finished their vows, they moved into St Edward's Chapel behind the altar to sign their marriage register, accompanied by immediate members of their family. Once the register had been signed, the couple walked out of the Abbey to Felix Mendelssohn's classic *Wedding March*.

Following the ceremony, the newlyweds left returned to Buckingham Palace. The wedding breakfast was held in the Ball-Supper Room at lunchtime, with a menu of "filet de sole Mountbatten, perdreau en casserole, and bombe glacée Princess Elizabeth". Elizabeth, taking into account the post-war rationing of food, only had 150 guests attending the wedding breakfast.

While the guests tucked into their food, they enjoyed the music provided by the string band of the Grenadier Guards. The delicate wedding favours were made from individual posies of myrtle and white heather, from the royal estate of Balmoral in Scotland.

The stunning wedding cake was made by McVitie and Price. It was nine-foot tall, separated into four tiers, made from ingredients that had been sent from all over the world. Even the sugar that was used had been provided by the Girl Guides in Australia, and as the result the cake was nicknamed 'The 10,000-Mile Cake'. The cake was decorated with the arms of the bride and groom's families, monograms of the bride and groom, sugar-iced figures of their favourite activities and also decorations of regimental and naval badges. Elizabeth and Philip cut the cake with the sword that had been gifted to the groom by his new father-in-law.

Although this was the couple's official wedding cake, the couple had received 11 wedding cakes in total. In fact, they received over 2,500 gifts and 10,000 telegrams of congratulations from well-wishers – Mahatma Gandhi had even sent a piece of cotton lace that he spun himself, embroidered with the words 'Jai Hind' or 'Victory for India' in English.

To greet those who had gathered on the Mall, Elizabeth and Philip made their way onto the balcony and waved to the adoring crowds. The next day, Elizabeth's wedding bouquet was sent back to Westminster Abbey to be laid on the Tomb of the Unknown Warrior, a royal tradition that had been started by her own mother.

The wedding fever that had consumed Britain did not end once the special day was over. Elizabeth's dress was exhibited at St James's Palace before embarking on a tour across the country, giving the public an opportunity to view it up close. The palace also exhibited all of the gifts that the couple had received for the public to enjoy, while cinemas held screenings of the wedding ceremony across the country.

A couple of years into their marriage, Philip relinquished his beloved and promising naval career to support his wife, as she assumed more responsibility in the wake of her father's declining health, proving to all that he would be a reliable consort to Elizabeth.

In 2007, Elizabeth became the first British monarch to celebrate a diamond wedding anniversary and in 2017, the royal couple reached their platinum anniversary. Over 70 years have passed since their magical wedding that lifted the spirit of the nation, and Elizabeth and Philip have proven that love can, indeed, last a lifetime.

Crowds of people gathered outside of Buckingham Palace to see the bride and groom

THE PRINCE OF HOPE

The birth of Prince Charles brought huge joy to his family, but his early years would see several separations from his mother and father

I f the marriage of the heir to the throne, Princess Elizabeth, to Prince Philip in 1947 had been billed as a celebration for Britain after years of wartime austerity, then the arrival of the couple's first child just under 12 months later was an added moment of sparkle for a country still dealing with the aftermath of war. However, the birth of this prince was also a pivotal moment for his family. A decade after the Abdication Crisis had called the very future of the monarchy into question, the House of Windsor was given a renewed strength by his birth, which secured the succession into the 21st century.

The royal wedding of 1947 had been a turning point for the royal family, and in the months that followed Elizabeth and Philip became the most celebrated members of the House of Windsor. An official trip to Paris in 1948 provided more glamour, but it also led to rumours that the princess was pregnant. She appeared pale and tired at an event, and her husband whisked her out of one room so that she could rest. In June, Buckingham Palace announced that the heir to the throne wouldn't be carrying out any more engagements from the end of that month - the rather discreet way that royal pregnancies were confirmed in the post-war years.

Elizabeth and Philip prepared for the arrival of their baby at Buckingham Palace, where they had been living for most of 1948. The young couple intended to move into Clarence House, but it was still undergoing major repairs while their planned country home, Sunninghill Park, had been hit by fire. So the expectant parents passed the final months of Elizabeth's pregnancy with King George VI and Queen Elizabeth, who helped oversee the plans for the birth of their first grandchild.

They also had to negotiate the way the new arrival would be known. Although Elizabeth was heir to the throne, her baby would take its title from its father, as only male-line grandchildren of a sovereign were automatically given royal status. Just days before the baby was born, King George VI ensured that his first grandchild would be royal from the moment of birth by issuing new Letters Patent, which confirmed the baby would hold the rank of HRH and the title of prince or princess.

A delivery room was set up in the Belgian Suite of Buckingham Palace. Named in honour of Queen Victoria's influential uncle, King Leopold of the Belgians, its three rooms were decorated with art by Canaletto and Gainsborough and among the pictures hanging on its walls were portraits of King George III and Queen Charlotte. The princess would end up spending several days there. Her labour began in the afternoon of Saturday 13 November 1948, but proved long and difficult.

Prince Philip, like many expectant fathers of the time, was kept outside the delivery suite, and as the labour progressed into a second day, he took his anxiety out on the squash court. It was there that he heard news of the birth, which cemented the House of Windsor's hold on the throne. The longed-for baby was born on 14 November 1948, after a 30-hour labour that ended with a Caesarean section, which had been carried out under general anaesthetic. However, the difficult delivery had been made easier by the decision to stop the practice that required the home secretary to be present to ensure the baby wasn't switched for another. Elizabeth gave birth safely and privately to her son at 9.14pm.

The baby was eventually delivered in the Buhl Room of Buckingham Palace, weighing 7lb 6oz and in perfect health. Prince Philip immediately opened champagne to start the toasts and was on hand with flowers for his wife when she eventually came round from her sedation.

The large crowd that had gathered outside for news of the royal birth had to wait a little longer to start their celebrations. The official announcement was pinned to the gates of Buckingham Palace just before midnight, and not long afterwards the arrival of the royal baby was broadcast on radio news bulletins.

In the hours after the baby prince's birth, thousands of telegrams poured into Buckingham Palace offering congratulations from around the world. Bonfires were lit around the country to celebrate the arrival of a future monarch, following a tradition that had been kept for centuries. Outside the palace the

THE PRIVATE BIRTH OF A PRINCE

For centuries politicians witnessed the heir's birth, but Elizabeth would give birth without them

As final preparations were made for the arrival of the longed-for heir, the home secretary, James Chuter Ede, was expected to attend the delivery to ensure that the baby wasn't substituted at the moment of birth. However, the idea seemed increasingly unnecessary and intrusive. When it was pointed out that a 1931 law meant that up to seven ministers from different parts of the empire might have to attend, King George VI decided to bring the tradition to an end once and for all.

It meant that Prince Charles became the first royal baby born without the presence of a politician for hundreds of years. Official witnesses to a royal birth had been compulsory since the end of the 17th century after the Protestant enemies of the Catholic King James II claimed that the healthy baby boy born to his queen in 1688 was actually a changeling.

Since then, queens and princesses had given birth with politicians in attendance. Queen Victoria decided in 1894 that just the home secretary would attend. By the early 20th century, he was usually in a discreet position outside the door to allow the royal mother a degree of privacy, but he was still required to attend all deliveries.

The ending of this royal tradition in 1948 meant that the last baby to be born in the presence of a politician was Princess Alexandra of Kent. The House of Windsor's future monarch had begun modernising from the moment of Prince Charles' birth.

Elizabeth and Philip photographed with Charles and Anne

James Chuter Ede, home secretary between 1945 and 1951, was told with just weeks to spare that his presence wouldn't be required for the birth of the heir to the throne's baby

crowds sang and partied into the small hours until they were asked to keep their celebrations quieter to allow mother and baby to get some rest.

The new second-in-line to the throne was soon ensconced in a nursery next to his mother's bedroom and spent his early weeks in quiet seclusion while the outside world continued to fete him with traditional gun salutes and peals of bells. Elizabeth was overjoyed with her son, writing to her aunt, May Elphinstone, that the baby was "too sweet for words", adding that she could hardly believe she had a son of her own. Her mother, Queen Elizabeth, described her grandson as a "darling" baby. The little prince's other grandmother, Princess Alice, was living in Greece at the time of his birth and heard about his arrival in a telegram from her son. Her sister, Queen Louise of Sweden, also wrote to her, affectionately describing the infant prince as having "a little bit

of fair fluff for hair". However, the outside world was kept waiting for a glimpse of the heir, with the first official portraits taken by royal favourite Cecil Beaton on 14 December, exactly a month after his birth. But even then there was no name to go with the face - that was to be kept a closely guarded secret until the day of his christening.

On 15 December 1948, the archbishop of Canterbury, Geoffrey Fisher, baptised the second in line to the throne as Charles Arthur Philip George. The baby had been carried into the service in the Music Room at Buckingham Palace wearing the Honiton lace christening gown first used by Queen Victoria and Prince Albert for their children. Fisher used water from the River Jordan for the baptism itself, which took place, as was traditional, at the gilded silver Lily Font.

The prince, born to be king, was supported by eight godparents at his christening, among them two reigning monarchs. His godfathers included his proud grandpa King George VI, King Haakon VII of Norway, as well as Prince George of Greece, and his great-uncle David Bowes-Lyon, the younger brother of Queen Elizabeth. His godmothers were led by his great-grandmother Queen Mary, while his aunt, Princess Margaret, also stood sponsor. Philip's grandmother Victoria, Dowager Marchioness of Milford Haven was another godmother, with his cousin Patricia Brabourne completing the line up.

His Royal Highness Prince Charles of Edinburgh, as he was officially known, spent his first Christmas with his family at Sandringham. However, the New Year would bring big changes for the little prince. In July 1949, Clarence House was finally ready for its new residents after an extensive refurbishment programme led by the duke of Edinburgh, which had drawn some criticism when it went over budget. So Charles left his grandparents' home at Buckingham Palace to move just round the corner with his parents. However, his parting from George VI and Elizabeth wouldn't last long.

The king's health had been giving cause for concern for some time. Two days before the birth of the boy who now stood to one day inherit his throne, George VI had been diagnosed with arteriosclerosis, which was so severe his doctors were concerned he might lose a leg. He had determined to keep his condition secret from Princess Elizabeth while she had her baby but shared the news soon afterwards. After she had recovered from her difficult delivery, his heir found herself taking on more of her father's duties. Meanwhile, Prince Philip, who had longed to return to active service, had been made second in command of Chequers, part of the Mediterranean fleet. He left for Malta with his wife following him not long afterwards. The baby Prince Charles was left with his grandparents.

Much of his day-to-day care was carried out by his nanny, Helen Lightbody, who was brought in to look after the little prince when he was a month old. Then aged 30, she had previously worked for the duke and duchess of Gloucester, supervising their two sons, Prince William and Prince Richard. Born in Scotland, she was known for her stern approach, which would later earn her the nickname 'No Nonsense Lightbody'. Her disciplined nursery became the centre of the young prince's world, and she was often seen pushing him through London's parks in his pram.

Charles was also cared for by Mabel Anderson, who joined the royal household as an under nanny in 1949. She was far more relaxed and fun than her stentorian boss, and the two women became important figures in the young prince's life. However, it was Queen Elizabeth who really took Charles under her wing. She clearly loved playing and spending time with her grandson and took charge of ensuring each birthday and Christmas he spent away from his parents was filled with many special moments to remember.

Years later, Prince Charles would talk about how his mother didn't spend as much time with him as he wished and their first separation - as she headed to Malta - was longer than first anticipated as Princess Elizabeth decided to extend her stay and enjoy Christmas on the island. When she returned at the start of 1950, she spent several days in London catching up on her work before heading to Sandringham, where the toddler prince had spent Christmas with his grandparents.

Although it was usual for upper-class families to spend time apart from their children, some US media reports criticised Elizabeth for her extended stays away after she headed back to Malta that spring for another break with her husband. When she returned she was in the early stages of her second pregnancy and back home there were more calls on her time. As the health of George VI continued to cause concern, there were more responsibilities

"THE CROWDS SANG AND PARTIED INTO THE SMALL HOURS"

Charles' early years were filled with family fun - here, aged around two, he plays hide-and-seek with his mother

A young Prince Charles poses with his grandmother, Queen Elizabeth. The two shared a very close bond

"SOME REPORTS CRITICISED ELIZABETH FOR HER EXTENDED STAYS AWAY"

for his heir to take on, but she was also able to pass happy days with her baby son, who was soon to become a big brother.

However, Prince Philip was still in Malta and only returned to England in July 1950 to await the birth of the new baby. Princess Anne arrived on 15 August that year in a far more straightforward delivery that took place at Clarence House. Now in command of the frigate Magpie, Philip travelled back and forth between England and Malta in the following months, leaving for another extended stay after the christening of his daughter. Charles, who now shared his nursery with a sister, waved goodbye again to his mother in November as she headed out to join Philip. Although still young, the

prince was spending increasingly less time with his parents and relying more and more on his grandmother, Queen Elizabeth.

The time he did spend with Philip would grow tense as the duke of Edinburgh saw how sensitive Charles could be and tried to train it out of him by encouraging him to brush off problems in the same practical way that he himself had always found so effective. It would cause friction between the two men in later years and even in early childhood. Philip was as likely to tell his young son to pick himself up and dust himself off as he was to offer cuddles and kisses after a tumble.

However, he was also a fun father, initiating hours of fun and games while he was at home. He was also quite clearly the head of their household, taking the lead in family matters even though his

The birth of a king in waiting was announced with the traditional, simple bulletin pinned to the gates of Buckingham Palace

Princess Elizabeth and Prince Philip pose with Prince Charles and Princess Anne at Buckingham Palace in October 1950

wife's role as queen-in-waiting was rapidly taking on more significance.

In October 1951, Elizabeth's position as heir took the couple to Canada and the United States for an official tour that would keep them away from home for over a month and cause them to miss their son's third birthday. On their return to England, Charles was waiting for them at Euston station with his grandmother but had to take second place to the formalities, receiving a kiss from his mother and a pat on the head from his father after they had greeted Queen Elizabeth.

It was in another moment of separation that Prince Charles' childhood changed forever. His mother was in Kenya when, on 6 February 1952, her father died in his sleep and she became queen. Her son was now heir to the throne, with a new

title of duke of Cornwall and a role that beckoned for him after a childhood that had started in the bliss of a cosy family life but had also entailed plenty of painful separations.

Soon after the birth of Prince Charles, his grandmother, Queen Elizabeth, wrote that "something as happy and simple and hopeful for the future as a little son is indeed a joy". As the House of Windsor contemplated a new era with yet more change to come, Charles remained the great joy of his family's life.

But, as the heir they had always desired from Princess Elizabeth, Charles was also the Windsors' great hope for the future. With that came a great burden of responsibility that would soon come to weigh heavily on the young prince's shoulders.

The last summer of King George VI saw young Charles spend sunny days with his beloved grandparents

BEYOND THE GILDED CAGE
ELIZABETH'S MALTESE YEARS

In 1949 Prince Philip's naval career called him to the Mediterranean but his young wife was determined to turn the situation to advantage. For a few years, getaways to Malta offered the princess glimpses of a relatively carefree life, largely unencumbered by the burdens of royal duty

Words **Jon Wright**

Malta had suffered terribly during the war. For the policy-makers, both Allied and Axis, the island was held in the highest strategic esteem. For the local people this meant privation, isolation and long periods under siege. The bombs fell, the horizon was crammed with menacing ships, and it was not for nothing that George VI awarded the entire island the George Cross in recognition of its bravery. Rebuilding would not be easy (though Britain quickly pledged to raise £30 million to that end), but the island had every chance of regaining its reputation as a haven of relaxation and quirky natural beauty.

Such, at least, must have been the hope of one of the world's most famous married couples. Perhaps the island would cast the spell with which it had once, long ago, enticed the poet Samuel Taylor Coleridge during his spell as secretary to Malta's first British governor. The place could be sweltering, Coleridge admitted, but because of the breeze he "never once found the heat oppressive". Visitors grumbled about the sirocco winds blowing in from North Africa but it was "a mere joke compared with our close, drizzly weather in England". All told, the "climate to me appears heavenly" and, Coleridge gleefully reported, he was "scarcely ever ill and very seldom... troubled with distressful dreams". Malta had changed – a little busier, now, with a population of roughly 350,000 – but perhaps it was still just

the sort of spot for Philip and Elizabeth to find some respite: he from the day's exertions aboard ship and she from the scrutiny and stuffiness of courtly life in England.

Early in the marriage, Philip's naval commitments had usually allowed for a 'home for dinner' lifestyle; work at the Admiralty or at the Naval Staff College in Greenwich only required small commutes. He was, however, itching for a

more dynamic role and this arrived in the autumn of 1949 when he was appointed as first lieutenant in the Mediterranean fleet, based at Malta, and second in command of HMS Chequers. The king was a little iffy about the posting, conscious that his failing health would require ever-increasing involvement by Philip and Elizabeth in royal duties. But Philip was unlikely to be deterred. He and Elizabeth both knew that a time would

Crowds on Gozo, Malta's sister island, cheer the prince and princess during a drive through the capital, Victoria, in April 1951

73

come - probably sooner than later - when the role of consort would make active military duty impossible. Philip was keen to make use of his training while he still could.

He arrived in Malta in October 1949 and took up residence in the Villa Guardamangia, a property in Valletta hired by Lord Mountbatten, who was also serving in the fleet as commander of the cruiser squadron. The frantic activity of the war years was over but the fleet still had important duties to perform: in Philip's case, this often involved goodwill/quasi-diplomatic trips to, among other places, Jordan, Turkey, Egypt and Iran - especially after he took command of his own vessel. It was also an era of social tension on the island. Britain was struggling with the question of what resources to commit to its naval operations in Malta and this provoked worries among the local population. 42 per cent of all employment on the island was related to the British military presence as late as 1954 and, as recently as 1948, talk of lay-offs at the naval dockyards had triggered serious strikes.

Philip wisely remained aloof from such issues and awaited the visits of his wife. Elizabeth

Princess on deck: Elizabeth poses with Philip and his fellow officers onboard HMS Chequers in December 1949

spent four periods on the island over the next three years. The first trip began on 20 November 1949. Elizabeth travelled without her young son, Charles, but spending Christmas with Philip and the Mountbattens seemed to help ease tensions between uncle and nephew - the relationship between the two men was always a little spiky. As for Elizabeth, Mountbatten was instantly smitten. The princess, he told his daughter, was "quite

enchanting and I've lost whatever of my heart is left to spare entirely to her. She dances quite divinely and always wants a samba when we dance together".

A leisurely time was had watching polo at the Marsa sports ground and making a splash on the island's party circuit before Elizabeth returned home on 28 December: Philip was scheduled to head out on patrols of the Red Sea. The princess was not away from Malta for long, enjoying a brief visit between 28 March and 9 May 1950, the highlight of which was the celebration of Elizabeth's 25th birthday on 21 April. The predictable swanky party filled the evening hours but, earlier in the day, Lord Mountbatten had ordered his flag captain Peter Howes to assemble a makeshift choir and band on HMS Liverpool to sing the traditional birthday greeting over the telephone to a puzzled but delighted princess. It was soon time to prepare for the birth of Elizabeth's second child, Anne, and trudge back to England.

Exciting news arrived from Malta in July. Philip had been granted command of his own ship (the frigate HMS Magpie) but taking up the reins had to be delayed so that he could hot-foot it to Britain for his daughter's arrival in August. He was back on the island by September and was joined by his wife at the first opportunity. This was to be the longest of Elizabeth's Maltese sojourns, stretching from 25 November 1950 to 12 February 1951.

The princess received some criticism in the press for, once again, leaving her children in the care of their grandparents over Christmas but, in fairness, they were rather young to travel and, while not a person of showy maternal affection, there is no question of her love for Charles and Anne. She proudly inflicted home movies and photos of Charles on her Maltese friends while Charles was able to develop close bonds with his grandmother that would long endure.

It is difficult to gauge how Elizabeth looked upon these Maltese days. Her cousin Margaret Rhodes concluded that the "happiest time for her must have been her very early married years... when she was just a naval wife in Malta... leading

"THE PRINCESS RECEIVED CRITICISM FOR LEAVING HER CHILDREN IN THE CARE OF THEIR GRANDPARENTS"

Husband and wife enjoy time on the island

Elizabeth attends a dance at the Hotel Phoenecia along with members of the Mediterranean Fleet's top brass

The inimitable Valletta skyline

BRONZES NOT BALLOT BOXES
Maltese politics were edging towards the chaotic, but Elizabeth managed to remain above the fray

In late 1951, Malta's prime minister, Giorgio Borg Olivier, presented Elizabeth with a miniature version of one of Valletta's most famous statues, Antonio Sciortino's *Les Gavroches* (*The Street Urchins*). The ceremony took place at the Auberge d'Aragon, a building that Elizabeth will have known well. Erected as a base for the Aragonese-speaking contingent of the Knights of the Order of St John during the 16th century, it was the only knightly auberge that had not been restored or destroyed. One of the island's unspoiled treasures, it now served as the prime minister's office.

A relationship was naturally sustained between Elizabeth and the local government, though of a rather less formal nature than back home in Britain. This slightly stand-offish approach was appropriate. Malta held elections at a frantic rate during the post-war years, with the Nationalist Party (damaged at first for its pro-Italian stance during the early 1940s) and the Labour Party (which had a rare gift for breaking up into factions).

The issue of Malta's future relationship with Britain was often a hotly debated topic and Elizabeth's name could easily have become embroiled. Fortunately, the princess's encounters with Malta's political leaders were more about watching polo matches together, being treated to occasional formal dinners, and receiving rather impressive pieces of art.

Antonio Sciortino's famous statue; a miniature version was presented to Elizabeth by the Maltese prime minister as a memento

an absolutely normal life". Normal is, of course, a relative term and it is not the average navy wife who turned up on her first visit to her husband with 40 cases of clothes, a small but significant retinue (headed by lady-in-waiting Alice Egerton) and a plain-clothes detective who followed her every move. Not many navy wives were expected to entertain foreign dignitaries - including the French president and the kings of Norway and Denmark - when they came to town. Mike Parker, Philip's private secretary, was a little more accurate when he explained that the pressures of royal status were much diminished but never entirely absent: Elizabeth "spent only ten per cent of her time being a princess".

Given what was to come, however, that was not a bad ratio. For the most part, Elizabeth did experience a welcome sense of freedom: doing the shopping with actual bank notes in her handbag, popping into the hairdressers or the cinema. She was even allowed, on occasion, to drive herself around the island. She enjoyed her nights at the

Saddle Club balls, the spectacle of her husband growing increasingly proficient at polo, and hosted a fair few cocktail and beach parties of her own. The acclaimed clarinetist Freddie Mizzi performed at several of these shin-digs and he recalled that "she and the duke used to dance a lot; she was also always so beautiful and always so nice and kind". The couple, he remembered, often insisted on their favourite tune being played: 'People Will Say We're in Love' from *Oklahoma*.

Elizabeth's mother reputedly summed up this era very well. It was a story of the little bird flying free then returning back home to its gilded cage. All too soon, the cage door closed for the last time. Elizabeth's final trip to Malta took place between 11 March and 9 April 1951. By that time, the king's health was rapidly deteriorating and Elizabeth was eager, as well as duty bound, to return home. It was a turning point for Philip, too. He would have to be by his wife's side and, in July, his active military service came, for all intents and purposes, to an end. The crew of the Magpie gave him a good send off and Philip proudly announced: "I have kept my promise to make HMS Magpie one of the finest ships in the fleet. The past 11 months have been the happiest of my sailor life." It was a justified comment. Philip had worked hard and the Magpie had been more than, as the detractors sometimes sniped, "the duke's private yacht".

Philip was noticeably edgy back in London. His valet John Dean recalled that "the duke was inclined to be moody and impatient when we first came home from Malta". On one occasion Philip caught a glimpse of his naval white uniform and commented, rather ruefully, that "it will be a long time before I want those again". And the 'want', of course, meant 'require' not 'desire'. Adjusting to life

on civvy street, even at one of the most fashionable addresses in the land, was never going to be easy for Philip but, of course, he buckled down. So there the royal couple were in July 1951, palace-dwellers surrounded by the grandest chinaware and sunk in the plushest armchairs, not sure what would happen next. It would only take a tragically brief time for them to find out.

ASCENT

THE DEATH OF GEORGE VI

He may have steered his country through the chaos of World War II,
but the stress took its toll on Britain's beloved monarch

Members of the public lined the street
to pay their respects to their king

It was 6 February 1952. The king's valet, James McDonald, was up bright and early to attend to his majesty. As usual, he started to prepare a bath for the king, knowing that the running water would be enough to wake him. But as the bath continued to fill up and the telltale signs of the king's footsteps could not be heard, McDonald's heart sank. Entering the king's bedroom to see a lifeless body, he rushed to get the doctor, who confirmed his fears - King George had died in his sleep.

Plagued with health problems and a heavy smoker for most of his life, George had been in decline for quite some time. His arteries had hardened and he had to give up a number of public appearances due to severe pain in his right leg and foot, caused by Buerger's disease. In fact, George almost lost his right leg due to an arterial blockage and had to be given a lumbar sympathectomy in March 1949.

George's poor health, as well as his smoking habit, had been exacerbated due to the stress of World War II and the post-war years. He had led his country admirably and along with his family had become a symbol of hope during the dark times of war. But it was a lot to deal with, particularly for a naturally anxious man who had reluctantly agreed to bear the crown.

Following the issues with his right leg, George's tour to Australia and New Zealand had to be postponed. It was decided that the tour should be rearranged so that George's eldest daughter and heir, Princess Elizabeth, could go instead with her husband, Prince Philip. As the king's health increasingly declined, Elizabeth began to take on a lot more responsibility to support her father, who she absolutely adored.

However, the worst was yet to come. In May 1951, the king was able to open the Festival of Britain, but it was painfully clear that he was unwell. He underwent X-rays that revealed a shadow had developed on his left lung. Hoping to avoid alarming the king, his doctors told him that he was suffering with a mild form of pneumonia, which could be treated with penicillin injections.

The next month, Princess Elizabeth attended the Trooping of the Colour on behalf of her father while he tried to recover from his illness. Yet over the coming months it became evident the king was suffering from something far worse than a bout of treatable pneumonia. After more tests it was confirmed that a malignant tumour had been found in George's left lung. It was recommended to the king that he undergo an operation to have the affected lung completely removed.

George felt uneasy about going under the knife, but his doctors assured him that it was the best possible treatment. To prevent him and the rest of his family from becoming even more anxious, they claimed that 'structural changes' necessitated the removal of the lung, rather than admitting that it was, in fact, cancer.

For the operation, a makeshift operating theatre was constructed on the first floor of Buckingham Palace, complete with an operating table, lighting and other surgical equipment. It was the best way to keep the king's condition under wraps and to

The streets of London were filled with people wishing to pay their respects to the king

King George pictured at London Airport a week before his untimely death at Sandringham

ensure he had privacy during the operation, which was conducted on the 23 September 1951.

The operation was led by Clement Price Thomas, who was ultimately made a Knight Commander of the Royal Victoria Order for his service to the king. George had been injected with anaesthetic inside his own room before he was wheeled to the theatre. While his left lung was successfully removed, the doctors' worst fears were confirmed during the operation - the cancer had also spread to the king's right lung. At best, George had a year to live.

Although the prognosis was not good, George's doctors resisted telling him the devastating news that he was suffering with lung cancer. The only person who appeared to work it out was the king's close friend and former prime minister Winston Churchill, who deduced the gravity of George's illness after discussing the matter with his own doctor. In the meantime, George concentrated on his recovery, attempting to get out of bed for a few minutes each day to improve his poor circulation.

By October, the king was still unwell. Unable to leave his bed to attend the Privy Council, a small delegation of the councillors gathered around his bedroom door in order to conduct business. As for Princess Elizabeth, she journeyed to Canada for a month-long tour, which had already been postponed because of her father's illness. With concern rising about the king's condition, Elizabeth's private secretary, Martin Charteris, carried with him a draft Accession Declaration and a message to the Houses of Parliament, just in case George died while they were away.

"AFTER MORE TESTS IT WAS CONFIRMED THAT A MALIGNANT TUMOUR HAD BEEN FOUND"

The Queen Mother (George's widow), the new queen, Elizabeth II, and Princess Margaret in mourning

© Getty

George restored public faith in the monarchy after his brother sparked the abdication crisis in 1936

Pictured in 1948, the toll of WWII and his smoking habit had physically aged the king beyond his years

Princess Elizabeth started taking on more and more responsibility as her father's health began to falter

A MOVING TRIBUTE

Churchill remembered his close friend King George in one of the most emotional speeches of his life

Originally disliking one another, the friendship between King George and Winston Churchill had developed during the turbulent years of World War II. They famously met in private once a week in order to discuss any developments in the war while enjoying a spot of lunch together.

Churchill had known for some time that George was dying. The day after George's death, he travelled to London Airport to greet his new sovereign, Queen Elizabeth, as she returned from Kenya. On the way there he dictated a speech, which would be broadcast that afternoon, in honour of his friend and king. According to one of his secretaries, the iron-willed Churchill was "in a flood of tears".

Churchill's emotional eulogy has gone down in history as one of his most eloquent speeches. In one particular passage, Churchill spoke of the king's illness and declared, "The last few months of King George's life, with all the pain and physical stresses that he endured - his life hanging by a thread from day to day, and he all the time cheerful and undaunted, stricken in body but quite undisturbed and even unaffected in spirit - these had made a profound and an enduring impression and should be a help to all."

His words, a tribute to his dear friend, perfectly summed up the difficulties that King George had bravely faced in his final years. With an uneasy start, Churchill would soon develop a close relationship with Elizabeth, mentoring her through the first three years of her reign until his retirement in 1955.

The king and Winston Churchill became firm allies after the latter's election as prime minister

The king's spirits were lifted when Churchill was elected as prime minister once again on 25 October, and he seemed to be improving. By 14 November he was well enough to attend Prince Charles' third birthday, and that December George was able to pre-record his annual Christmas broadcast for that year. He then travelled to Sandringham for Christmas with his family, even managing to enjoy a few rounds of shooting across his estate.

As the end of January approached, Princess Elizabeth and Prince Philip were preparing to head out on a tour of Australia and New Zealand via Kenya. The tour had long been in the works and the original plan had been for George and his wife, Queen Elizabeth, to go, but the king was still not well enough to travel. Even so, nothing would stop George from seeing his daughter off at London Airport on 31 January, despite medical advice that he should not go.

George's appearance at the airport was the last time he would be seen by the public. He spent his final days at Sandringham, and on 5 February, the day before his death, George enjoyed what would be his last day of shooting. His footman, Daniel Long, had taken a warm cup of cocoa up to the king at 11pm, not realising that he would be the last one to see George alive. At 7.30am the next morning, George was found dead in his bed after suffering a coronary thrombosis (a blood clot to the heart) during in his sleep. He was only 56.

Just over an hour since George had been declared dead, the codeword for his passing, 'Hyde Park Corner', was triggered by his principal private secretary, Sir Alan Lascelles. When Churchill was informed of the 'bad news' he blustered, "Bad news? The worst!" As the seriousness of the king's health had not been made known to the public, his death came as a shock to many.

Sadly, one of the last people to discover the news of George's passing was Princess Elizabeth, who had spent the night at the remote Treetops Hotel in Kenya observing wildlife. Upon receiving the news she hastily returned home with the rest of the royal party - at 25 years old, she was now the new queen of the United Kingdom.

As news of the king's death swept the country, Union Jacks were flown at half-mast, shops and factories were closed for the day and members of the public began to arrive outside Buckingham Palace to mourn. George's coffin was kept at St Mary Magdalene Church, Sandringham, for two days before it travelled to London via train and subsequently moved to Westminster Hall to lie in state from 11 February, where more than 300,000 people arrived to get one last glimpse of their highly respected king.

George's funeral was held on 15 February at St George's Chapel at Windsor Castle, with his body interred in the Royal Vault. The Government sent a wreath - made from white and lilac carnations - in the shape of the George Cross, the award founded by George, with the phrase 'For Valour' written on a card by Churchill. In 1969, George's body was transferred from the Royal Vault to the King George VI Memorial Chapel, which was also located inside St George's Chapel.

After spending just over 15 years on the throne, George had successfully restored faith in the monarchy after the disastrous abdication of his brother, King Edward VIII. Remarkably, the funeral of George's youngest daughter, Princess Margaret, was held exactly 50 years later on 15 February, 2002. The royal family would suffer another tragedy when George's wife, remembered now as Queen Elizabeth, the Queen Mother, passed away just seven weeks later. Both of their remains were interred in the Memorial Chapel, reunited with their father, husband and Britain's endearing king.

© Getty

A spectacular view from the very top of Westminster Abbey down to the coronation theatre, where the Queen is about to be crowned

GLORIANA

The coronation of Elizabeth II took nearly 18 months to plan and was heralded as the beginning of a bright and promising new age for a country still beleaguered by post-war austerity

"What is the finest sight in the world?" Horace Walpole wrote to a friend after witnessing the crowning of Elizabeth II's ancestor George III in 1761. "A coronation". The hallowed walls of Westminster Abbey had witnessed six coronations, all of them with more than their fair share of drama, since that of George III in 1761.

Although each successive monarch imposed their own personality and wishes on the event, the solemn, ancient ceremony always remained essentially the same, employing regalia and following rituals that had been in use for several centuries. A stark example is the order of service laid out in the *Liber Regalis*, a precious 14th-century book that had most likely been written at the time of the crowning of Anne of Bohemia, consort of Richard III, and then used for all subsequent coronations.

Nonetheless, when Princess Elizabeth inherited the throne in February 1952, there were expectations that her coronation ceremony would be particularly impressive, with innovative touches that reflected the technological advances that had been made since her father's coronation, 16 years earlier in 1937. In the intervening years, Britain had been ravaged by war and although eight years had passed since the celebrations of VE Day, the nation had not yet fully recovered from its gruelling ordeal.

Much of London had been rebuilt, but many parts of the capital still looked sadly dilapidated and were riddled with ugly bomb sites, which served as a stark reminder of the horrors of the Blitz. Although food supplies were gradually

improving, the economy had not yet recovered and some aspects of rationing would remain in force until the summer of 1954.

Now that the euphoria and relief that followed the end of the war had died away, the general mood across the nation was bleakly despondent as people struggled to rebuild not just their homes, but also their lives, while at the same time dealing with the effects of the post-war economic austerity. The death of the universally beloved George VI at the beginning of 1952 only served to increase the gloom that pervaded the country, where the late king was respected and loved for his steadfast leadership during the war, and over 300,000 people patiently queued for hours in order to pay their respects when his coffin lay in state in Westminster Hall.

Preparations for the new monarch's coronation began almost immediately after the death of her father, although, as was traditional, it was expected that a decent mourning period of around a year and a half would elapse before the actual crowning took place. Although the death of the King George VI had been greeted with genuine sorrow, the accession of his daughter was regarded as a sign of better times to come, perhaps even a 'New Elizabethan Age' to rival that presided over by her namesake Elizabeth I who, coincidentally, had also been just 25 years old when she succeeded to the throne. Princess Margaret later described it as "like a phoenix time. Everything was being raised from the ashes".

To underline what was anticipated to be the beginning of a new golden age for Britain and its people, it was decided to hold the coronation the following summer. This was in the hope of

ensuring that the big day, which was chosen from a Met Office list predicting the most sunny days of the year, would have glorious sunshine - only for it to pour with rain and be one of the coldest June days on record.

Although the weather, as always, proved to be beyond human control, great efforts were made to ensure that every other aspect of the day went as smoothly as possible. The Coronation Commission, who were tasked with organising the event, met for the first time four months after George VI's death, with the duke of Edinburgh acting as chairman at the Queen's request.

According to tradition, unlike their female counterparts, male consorts of female rulers were not crowned alongside them during the coronation ceremony, which meant that Philip would not be consort. Conscious that her proud and energetic husband was already feeling rather ignored and sidelined by the establishment that surrounded her, the new queen was naturally keen to ensure that he was as involved as possible in the preparations for the ceremony.

Traditionally, the organisation of the coronation was presided over by the duke of Norfolk in his heredity capacity of Earl Marshal, which involved being in charge of all major royal ceremonies. Although the current duke retained full control of the arrangements, he would liaise with the duke of Edinburgh, who was already brimming with ideas and would prove to be an invaluable asset - although one of his first suggestions, that the ceremony be televised, immediately brought him into conflict with his wife and several others on the committee.

"AROUND 277 MILLION PEOPLE WATCHED THE CORONATION AROUND THE WORLD"

In 1952, just 14 per cent of UK households had a television set, with even more having access to one, and the number was set to rise even more over the next few years. For the duke of Edinburgh, keen to modernise and invigorate the institution of royalty, televising the coronation ceremony was a perfect opportunity to reinforce the relationship between crown and populace, by ensuring that his wife's subjects could feel like actual participants in the ceremony.

However, if he had expected the Queen to be in full agreement with his suggestion then he was about to be proved wrong. She strongly opposed the notion, feeling like it would be undignified for the sacred moment of crowning to be broadcast into people's sitting rooms, where they might not be behaving in a properly respectful manner. She was also aware that previous coronations had been riddled with mistakes, such as the famous incident when Queen Victoria's coronation ring was forced on to her finger despite being far too small for her, and had no wish for any gaffes to be witnessed by millions of viewers. She was backed by several members of cabinet and the archbishop of Canterbury, Geoffrey Fisher, who

considered television to be "potentially one of the greatest dangers of the world".

At first they prevailed, but the announcement in October 1952 that the ceremony would not be televised was greeted by such universal disappointment and dismay - the populace having become used to royal events being televised - that they were eventually forced to backtrack. However, at the Queen's request, there were to be no close-up shots of her face and certain parts of the ceremony, such as the anointing and Communion, would not be broadcast as they were considered to be too sacred.

On the day, over 27 million people watched the coronation in the UK, with an estimated 277 million watching worldwide thanks to sterling efforts by television companies who arranged that films of the event should be flown overseas as quickly and efficiently as possible, meaning that viewers in some countries were able to watch the coverage on the same day.

The unprecedented presence of television cameras presented new problems for the committees organising the event, particularly those tasked with liaising with Westminster Abbey, where the utmost care had to be taken to ensure that the building was returned to the exact same state once the event was at an end.

As part of the preparation, a large-scale model of Westminster Abbey was created to help officials plan the logistics of the day, which would involve increasing the normal seating capacity of the building from 2,100 to 7,500 and make enough space for what would ultimately amount to 8,251 guests. On top of this, they added a temporary annexe and all the facilities, such as 52 drinking water fountains, lavatories and even ten small sick bays, which were necessary to ensure the comfort and safety of such an enormous gathering of people.

The abbey closed to the public on the first day of 1953, which gave the organisers five months to

© Getty

Cecil Beaton's photographs of the Queen on her coronation day remain among some of the most iconic royal portraits in history

PRACTICE MAKES PERFECT

Organisers insisted that there should be several rehearsals before the big event

In the weeks before the big day, several rehearsals were carried out in Westminster Abbey in order to ensure that the coronation ceremony would be as perfect as possible. However, the Queen preferred to rehearse in private in the ballroom of Buckingham Palace and also spent several hours a day wearing the heavy St Edward's Crown, which weighed nearly five pounds, while she went about her business.

As the big day drew nearer, she quietly attended two of the dress rehearsals at Westminster Abbey, where the duchess of Norfolk acted as her stand in. The rehearsals not only gave everyone an opportunity to practise, but also pinpointed any issues that might cause problems on the day, particularly with a live broadcast.

An MP who attended one of the rehearsals reported that in his opinion, the Queen's maids of honour looked too pale under artificial light and recommended they apply makeup to appear more tanned so they wouldn't look washed out on television. On another occasion, the Earl Marshal decided that all the page boys looked too scruffy and ordered them to get haircuts, threatening to report them to their headmasters if they refused.

All of this preparation was felt to be worth it in the end, though, as the coronation itself passed almost without hitch - although there was an awkward moment at the end of the royal and state processions when the doors opened and everyone stood up, expecting the Queen, only for a group of cleaners to make an appearance and start vacuuming the carpet ready for the main procession, much to the audience's amusement and the horror of the archbishop of Canterbury.

Queen Elizabeth spent hours practising for her coronation as the robes and regalia were so heavy and difficult to manage

prepare the interior - a mammoth task that involved covering the floor with a temporary wooden floor, boarding over the monuments and then erecting scaffolding to build the many tiers of seating for the guests. Meanwhile the annexe was being erected, it having been decided that it should look modern rather than being constructed in a pseudo-gothic style that had been favoured in the past.

The coronation regalia, including the crown itself, were to be housed in the annexe until they were required. It was also fitted with robing rooms for the Queen and the duke of Edinburgh, and a kitchen that served refreshments to the royal family, attendants and numerous peers taking place in the processions.

Although the committees were keen for the ceremony and its setting to be as splendid as possible, they were always acutely aware that many of the population were still suffering the effects of post-war austerity and that they needed to be sensitive to this fact. In the end, the coronation was estimated to cost £1.57 million (around £40 million in 2019), which included the cost not just of the abbey's decoration, but also the processions to and from Buckingham Palace, stands for the spectators and street decorations.

While the Coronation Committee was working on the details of the service and complicated logistics of what would be one of the grandest royal ceremonies of the century, the Queen's favourite designer, Norman Hartnell, who had also designed her wedding dress in 1947, was working on her coronation gown.

Following Queen Elizabeth's direction, Hartnell submitted eight different designs in varying degrees of ornateness until she finally selected a white satin gown richly embroidered with the floral symbols of Great Britain and the Commonwealth, which were picked out in gold bullion thread and embellished with crystals and pearls. The gown took eight months to make and towards the end required three dressmakers and six embroiderers from the Royal School of Needlework to work around the clock to ensure it would be ready in time. As a final touch, Hartnell incorporated a tiny four-leaf clover on the left-hand side of the skirt, where the Queen's hand would brush against it during the ceremony.

Along with the coronation gown, Hartnell also designed the colobium sindonis, the traditional plain white linen dress that the Queen donned after her anointing along with the cloth of gold supertunica. But his work didn't stop there.

Hartnell also designed the satin gowns worn by her six maids of honour, who complained that they were extremely itchy as they had been left unlined, as well as a new robe for peeresses, who were required to wear a special crimson velvet robe trimmed with miniver to the ceremony. As the basic design for this garment had changed very little over the years, many women were able to wear robes that had been passed down through their families, but for those who were not fortunate to have one stored in the attic, buying a new one was an expensive necessity. Beneath their robes, they wore ball gowns and their most splendid jewels, although, clearly at least one of the peeresses attending the event was rather careless with her belongings as after the coronation was over, the cleaning staff found a discarded diamond necklace, which remained unclaimed for six weeks.

On 24 March 1953, Queen Elizabeth's formidable grandmother Queen Mary died in her sleep at the age of 85. There were just ten weeks to go before the coronation but any fears that it might have to be postponed were allayed when it was revealed that the late queen had stipulated in her will that it should go ahead as planned.

The presence of her eldest son, the former Edward VIII, now duke of Windsor, who had been visiting her in London at the time of her death, also caused some embarrassment to the royal family as, at the request of Queen Elizabeth, who did not want him there, he had not been invited to the coronation. When Edward asked Winston Churchill to intervene, the prime minister took the Queen's side and informed the former king that it would be inappropriate for him to attend and then advised him to issue a face-saving press release stating that he did not plan to be there, which the duke duly did, although with very poor grace.

When Edward was not invited to his Elizabeth's wedding in 1947, his sister, Princess Mary, had also refused to attend to show solidarity with her snubbed brother. This time, however, she accepted her invitation, and the royal family closed ranks in order to show support to the young ruler.

Queen Elizabeth arrives at Westminster Abbey for her coronation, carrying a bouquet of flowers like a bride to symbolise her wedding to her country

"THE GOWN TOOK EIGHT MONTHS TO MAKE"

Elizabeth also had huge amounts of support in the Houses of Parliament, where the coronation was universally regarded as a new, regenerative start for the nation, even if some Labour MPs expressed concern about the cost of such an event at a time of austerity. The press were also enthusiastic, particularly overseas, where Queen Elizabeth was a very popular figure thanks to her youth, prettiness and royal glamour. In the run-up to the coronation and immediately afterwards, newspapers and magazines were filled with stories and articles about the Queen and her family as the pageant and glitter of the coronation dispelled the last lingering impression that Britain, once one

THE OFFICIAL PHOTOGRAPHS
Cecil Beaton's photographs of the Queen in her coronation regalia are among the most iconic and familiar royal portraits in history

Although the duke of Edinburgh had expressed a wish that his friend, the society photographer Baron, who had taken his wedding photos, should be awarded the honour of taking the official photographs to mark the Queen's coronation, he was swiftly overruled by his wife and her mother, both of whom insisted that the job had to go to Cecil Beaton. Excited and thrilled to be asked, Beaton

began to prepare several months in advance by ordering two enormous backdrops, one painted with the interior of Westminster Abbey's beautiful Lady Chapel, for the Queen to pose in front of in the temporary studio set up in Buckingham Palace's Green Drawing Room.

Aware that the Queen was exhausted, Beaton tried to work as quickly as possible even though the

lighting was less than ideal and the duke of Edinburgh, still irked not to have got his own way, was bossing him about. At the end of the brief session, Beaton wasn't even sure that any of the photographs were useable and so was delighted and relieved when he discovered how well they had turned out despite the intense pressure that he had been under while taking them.

The duke of Edinburgh's behaviour exasperated Cecil Beaton while he was taking the official photographs

An official photograph of the Queen with her Mistress of the Robes and six maids of honour, who carried her train throughout the ceremony - a task that they found rather arduous as it was extremely heavy

H.M. THE QUEEN WITH HER MAIDS OF HONOUR.

An official invitation to the Queen's coronation, which was attended by 8,251 guests. Prince Charles received his own specially hand-painted invitation to his mother's big day

of the most powerful nations on Earth, was still languishing in a battered and beleaguered state almost a decade after the end of the war.

Coronation day started at dawn for the stewards tasked with preparing Westminster Abbey for the event and they were amused to find Matins, one of the abbey's cats, fast asleep on the Coronation Chair when they started to arrive. Elsewhere, the guests were rising early in order to get ready as they were expected to be in their seats by 8.30am. They had a long wait until the service began at 11.15am, with many smuggling in books, sandwiches, flasks of coffee and miniature bottles of gin, whisky and brandy to sustain them as they waited. One of the archbishops astounded a group of page boys by revealing that he had sandwiches concealed beneath his mitre. Many of the guests had with them that morning's newspapers, which proudly proclaimed that a British team of climbers led by Edmund Hillary had become the first men to successfully reach the summit of Everest.

When the Queen, who was wearing the George IV State Diadem, arrived at 11am, the Earl Marshal, armed with a clipboard, quickly organised her procession, which comprised 250 people who all needed to be marshalled into the correct places.

"Ready, girls?" the Queen asked her maids of honour as the organ began to play and they started to make their way towards the altar, where in her nervousness, she accidentally forgot to make the traditional curtsey. The rest of the ceremony passed without any serious mistakes and the guests watched in awe as the Queen was formally presented to the throng by the archbishop of Canterbury, receiving their shouts of acclaim with a curtsey.

During the early planning stage of the coronation, there had been some arguments about whether it was appropriate for the Queen to curtsey to her people - perhaps surprisingly, her husband had expressed the opinion that it was undignified for her to do so, while the Queen insisted that it was the right thing to do and, in the end, got her way.

After this, she then gravely took an oath upon the Bible to govern her people fairly, mercifully and without prejudice, after which she donned a plain white tunic and then, beneath a gold canopy held over her by four Knights of the Garter, was anointed with sweetly scented holy oil made to a formula first created for the coronation of Charles II in 1661.

After the anointing, the Queen knelt for a blessing and then donned the white robe and supertunica in order to be invested with the royal regalia and then, finally, crowned, with the front of St Edward's Crown helpfully marked with a tiny gold star on the velvet so that the archbishop would know which way to place it.

As soon as the crown was in place, the entire congregation shouted "God save the Queen", and the peers and peeresses donned their own coronets. The anointed and crowned young queen then proceeded to the throne, where she received the homage of her peers and leading churchmen, with the archbishop of Canterbury, as senior prelate of the Church of England, leading the way, followed by the duke of Edinburgh, who happily knelt before his wife and declared himself to be her "liege man of life and limb" before kissing her cheek. At one point

The royal family and their attendants gathered on the balcony of Buckingham Palace to watch a special RAF flypast over London

during the three-hour ceremony, the Queen glanced up at the balcony where her four-year-old son Prince Charles was watching, flanked by his grandmother and aunt, Princess Margaret, and smiled at him.

The ceremony ended with the new queen and her husband taking Communion before retreating into the chapel behind the altar screen in order to exchange the heavy St Edward's Crown for the less cumbersome Imperial Crown, don her new purple Robe of State and have a nip of brandy from a flask produced by one of the archbishops, before she solemnly led the procession back out of the abbey and into the annexe, where they were to rest and have lunch, which had the newly invented coronation chicken as one of the courses.

After lunch, which the Queen barely touched, the royal couple clambered back into the Gold State Coach for the return journey along a five-mile route to Buckingham Palace. The procession, which was two miles long and incorporated 46

"THE CROWD STRETCHED ALL ALONG THE MALL AS FAR AS TRAFALGAR SQUARE"

bands and 16,000 participants, as well as 30,000 members of the armed forces, took an hour and 40 minutes. The cumbersome royal carriage moved slowly enough for most of the many thousands who had patiently lined the route since early in the morning - many of them spending the previous night sleeping on the pavement to ensure that they got a good spot - to get a good glimpse of the Queen, who gamely smiled and waved for the entire trip.

Upon her return to the palace, Queen Elizabeth was immediately whisked off to have the official photographs taken by Cecil Beaton, who felt under pressure to produce his best work in the least possible time. After this, the entire royal family made their first appearance of the day on the famous balcony of Buckingham Palace, where they waved at an enormous, cheering crowd,

which stretched all along the Mall as far as Trafalgar Square.

There had been some who had questioned whether such an ancient and religious rite and associated celebration was appropriate for the modern age, but they were effectively silenced by the enthusiasm with which the coronation was received by the press and, most importantly, the populace. Even the Soviet Ambassador, Yakov Malik, representing a communist state, was noted to appear very moved by the service with, as one witness later recalled "a look on his face of a kind of sadness that this was something outside himself". For most, the coronation had transformed the country, increased their prestige overseas and, most importantly, given them hope for a brighter future with the second Queen Elizabeth standing proudly at the helm.

CORONATION GARB

Discover the ornate outfit that Elizabeth II wore to her ceremony

1. THE SCEPTRE
The Sovereign's Sceptre was made for the coronation of Charles II in 1661 and represents the monarch's temporal power at the head of the state. The 530-carat Cullinan I, the largest colourless cut diamond in the world, is mounted in the head of the sceptre.

2. CORONATION NECKLACE
Made for Queen Victoria in 1858 by Garrard & Co, the coronation necklace comprises 25 cushion diamonds with the 22.48-carat Lahore diamond as a pendant. Since 1902, it has been worn by every queen at their coronation and is one of the Queen's favourite pieces.

3. THE ORB
The Sovereign's Orb was made for the coronation of Charles II in 1661 and represents the Christian world. Made from solid gold and weighing 2.6 pounds, it is decorated with 375 pearls, 365 diamonds, 18 rubies, nine emeralds, nine sapphires, one amethyst and one piece of glass.

4. THE GOWN
The Queen's white satin gown was designed by Norman Hartnell and took eight months to create, using British silk, which was painstakingly decorated with the embroidered floral emblems of Britain and the Commonwealth and then embellished with thousands of diamanté, crystals and seed pearls.

5. THE IMPERIAL STATE CROWN
The current state crown was made by royal jewellers Garrard & Co in 1937 for the coronation of George VI and is modelled on a crown made for Queen Victoria. The silver, gold and platinum frame is decorated with 2,868 diamonds, 273 pearls, 17 sapphires, 11 emeralds and five rubies.

6. CORONATION EARRINGS
The coronation earrings were made for Queen Victoria in 1858, using diamonds retrieved from other pieces in the royal collection such as an old Order of the Garter badge. Since 1911, they have been traditionally worn by every queen at the coronation ceremony.

7. QUEEN ELIZABETH II'S ARMILLS
The Queen's solid gold ceremonial bracelets, known as armills, were a coronation gift from the Commonwealth and intended to replace the old pair, which had been in use since 1661. The bracelets represent sincerity and wisdom as well as being symbolic of the bond between the sovereign and their people.

8. THE ROBE OF STATE
Elizabeth II's heavy purple velvet Robe of State was specially made for her coronation by the royal robe makers Ede & Ravenscroft and follows strict guidelines which stipulate that the train should be six yards long, trimmed with ermine and decorated with gold embroidery.

ALL ABOARD THE WINDSOR EXPRESS!
THE COMMONWEALTH TOUR OF 1953/4

It was one the most ambitious odysseys ever undertaken by the British monarchy. Embarking upon a world-circling tour of the Commonwealth was as glamorous in theory as it was exhausting in practice, but the visits made a profound impression on the Queen and her subjects

Words **Jon Wright**

The Queen en route to the Sydney cenotaph during her stay in Australia

Between November 1953 and May 1954, the Queen and Prince Philip were to be found dashing through the Caribbean and Australasia then back home to Britain via the Pacific, Africa and the Mediterranean. An impressive 40,000 miles were traversed by plane, ship, train and a dazzling array of four-wheeled vehicles. Tens of millions of people managed to catch a glimpse of the royal couple.

The Commonwealth Tour was, however, much more than a succession of "meet your new queen" jamborees. In the post-imperial world this was a very delicate moment in the relationship between Britain and its overseas territories, and the ideal of a united family of allies was far from being a fait accompli. Recent losses, such as India and the Palestinian Mandate, cast a long shadow and, in many places, tough questions were being asked about the need for greater independence and fully realised local political initiative. Even the occasional republican rumbling could be detected.

The Commonwealth tour helped to calm these waters: the Queen encountered adulation, sometimes verging on the raucous, wherever she went. Upon Elizabeth's return to Britain, the Labour leader Clement Attlee told the House of Commons: "It is all very well to have a formula or to have a constitution or even a flag, but people want to feel a loyalty and affection towards people and see those people and know those people." It was an astute comment. Assuredly, the whirligig of history would soon bring in its surprises, but this was still an excellent way to kick off a reign.

From outpost to outpost

The tour began with a long-haul flight to Bermuda then a trip to Jamaica where the royal party rendezvoused with the royal yacht SS Gothic - the Queen's main base for the remainder of the trip. The pattern was quickly set: the cheering crowds, the photo-ops, the important but never overly earnest conversations with local leaders.

Even at this early stage, however, tensions were conspicuous. Jamaica went gaga for the Queen but, in the background, concerns about Britain's overly interventionist antics simmered away. In not-too-distant British Guinea, the radical-leaning People's Progressive Party had triumphed in the April 1953 elections. The British authorities declared a state of emergency, suspended the constitution, and established an interim government under the direct rule of the British governor. As some members of the Jamaican press pointed out, this was hardly a shining example of a democracy-loving Britain with its arbitrary days banished to the past.

The atmosphere was lacking any stress in the next ports of call. Fiji was kind enough to show off and make presents of its traditional and effortlessly elegant tapa mats, while in Tonga, Elizabeth was delighted to meet up with Queen Salote Tupou - who had made such a good impression at the

The Queen enjoys a slice of traditional life at Lautoka, Fiji

recent coronation - and award her the prestigious title of Dame Grand Cross of the Royal Victorian Order. Better yet, an air of informality crept into proceedings. A cosy meal of yams, lobsters, pork and coconut milk was served up, and Elizabeth and Philip, as Tongan tradition demanded, ate with their fingers while sitting on the floor.

These had all been fleeting visits - a couple of days at best - but the next major destination, New Zealand, would reveal just how carnivalesque a royal tour could become. One journalist announced that 23 December 1954 was the "day Auckland went wild with joy. Strong men wept. Dignified businessmen and their wives ran. Brown and white men stood arm in arm and cheered. Traffic police laughed. Constables smiled and joked."

"AS MUCH AS THREE-QUARTERS OF THE POPULATION MANAGED TO GOGGLE AT THE QUEEN"

As elsewhere, the New Zealand trip had overt political goals. Not so long ago, New Zealand had been sending vast quantities of milk products and meat to wartime Britain. Now, it was keen to demonstrate its vibrant economy, which explains the number of visits to agricultural sites and factories. New Zealand realised just how important Britain was to its financial well-being: in 1950, 66 per cent of its exports headed to the UK. Britain, meanwhile, knew New Zealand was pivotal to its plans for a coherent Commonwealth and the Queen went out of her way to portray herself as a dedicated ruler. She attended meetings of the privy council, opened Parliament, and laid the foundation stone of Wellington's new Anglican Cathedral. In her Christmas Day message, transmitted from

Auckland, she explained that she felt "completely and most perfectly at home" and promised that the Commonwealth "bears no resemblance to the empires of the past" and was "built on the highest qualities of the spirit of man: friendship, loyalty and the desire for freedom and peace".

The welcome in Auckland was followed by terrible news. On 24 December, a dam on Mount Ruapehu was breached and waters, rocks and mud from a crater lake flooded out, destroying a river-straddling railway bridge as one of their targets. A train was caught up in the mayhem at Tangiwai and 151 people were killed. New Zealand was in shock and during her Christmas Day message, Queen Elizabeth expressed her most profound condolences. In a way, this helped the nation to rally together and Prince Philip won great praise for disrupting the carefully planned royal itinerary to attend the state funeral of many of the victims.

Over the weeks, enthusiasm for the royal couple only soared. People would sleep outside to secure a prime vantage point and it was not unknown for farmers to paint their sheep red, white and blue. 46 towns and cities were included in the schedule along with 110 formal engagements. As much as three-quarters of the country's population managed to goggle at the Queen - even if this sometimes only amounted to picking out her face as she whizzed by in a motorcade.

The royals even made a decent fist of confronting the issue of Māori grievances. To its discredit, New Zealand society tended to regard the Māori as an exotic fringe group who were only really good for putting on dramatic dances. They were certainly low down on the pecking order when the royal tour was being planned. A short, formal visit was arranged at Rotorua

and, for a time, it was far from clear that a stop at Ngarauwahia, still less a meeting with the Māori king, was deemed worthwhile. In the end, three minutes were allotted. The Māori sustained great loyalty for the Crown, however, despite Britain's less than stellar performance in upholding the terms of the 1840 Waitangi treaty, which supposedly protected Māori rights. As things turned out, the royal party made the decision to do more than wave as they passed by Ngarauwahia. The cars stopped, the Queen stepped out, and spent 20 minutes with the king. It was a small, but deeply meaningful gesture.

Australia catches Elizabeth fever

The powers-that-be were genuinely concerned by the prospect, albeit slim, of vocal opposition to the Australian leg of tour. The country clearly had a burgeoning sense of becoming a major power in the sphere of Asian-Pacific politics and, on the far left, some increasingly bitter verbal onslaughts had been launched against the British monarchy.

In fact, no major kerfuffles blighted the trip and protests did not rise much above the level of a handful of communist politicians refusing to wear suits and ties during the festivities. Writing in the *Sydney Morning Herald* on 4 February 1954 the day after millions of people celebrated the Queen's

arrival, Prime Minister Robert Menzies offered a glowing report: when such crowds "spontaneously pour out this feeling they are engaging in a great act of common allegiance and common joy which brings them closer together and is one of the most powerful elements converting them from a mass of individuals to a great, cohesive nation."

Over the next two months the tour took in 57 towns and cities, involved 33 flights, and imposed a work load of up to five formal engagements per day. The royal party travelled as far north as Cairns, to Hobart in the south, and to the oppressive weather of the old mining town Broken Hill in the west. Formal events and receptions were par for the course - to hospitals and war memorials, to chat with high-ranking clerics and politicians - but the quirkier, lower-key encounters perhaps did a better job of capturing the feel of the tour.

There was nothing particularly swanky about the stop-off in the Melbourne suburb of Northcote on 4 March, but the locals had cobbled together as colourful a welcome as they could manage. The town hall was decorated with images of the Queen and duke, provided by the council's painter Fred Forde. Multicoloured lights were strung along the high street and local businessmen had set up a fancy-sounding Royal Visit Exhibition, though this was really just a room containing stands that

The small-town crowds come out in force during the Queen's visit to Huntly, New Zealand in January 1954

explained the cornerstones of the local economy. The humble nature of the trip - replicated across Australia - didn't matter a jot. The people of Northcote were rather proud to have raised the £150 required for decorations and they were rewarded by the sight of the Queen in a particularly striking emerald-coloured coat.

Soon enough, it was time to leave Australia behind. Ceylon proved to be something of a mixed bag. It was fun to celebrate the Queen's birthday (50,000 well-wishers launched into a rendition of the familiar birthday tune), nobody is going to grumble when invited to visit elephants in the wild, and Prince Philip seemed to have a particularly jolly time planting a commemorative bush in the Nuwara Eliya tea plantations.

Against all this, possible anti-royal agitation convinced Ceylon's prime minister that the trip

The Queen is greeted by dignitaries upon her arrival at Entebbe airport in Uganda

People at home in Britain were eager to follow the events of the tour and newspapers were keen to oblige

THE TRIAL RUNS

The great Commonwealth Tour was not the royal couple's first experience of flying the flag abroad. One earlier odyssey had been a roaring success; another trip had been cut short by family tragedy

In the autumn of 1951, King George VI's declining health made a long-planned tour of Canada impossible. Elizabeth and Philip were obliged to stand in. The ensuing 35-day trip (beginning on 8 October) saw Elizabeth and Philip sweep from coast to coast, with cities like Toronto, Ottawa, Quebec and Montréal competing to stage the most grandiose receptions.

As with the later Commonwealth tour, the formal and the informal sat side by side. By day it was a visit to Parliament or a tour of an oil refinery; by night it was attendance at a hockey game or square dancing (with authentic clothing) at Ottawa's Rideau Hall. The trip concluded with a dash southwards to meet with President Truman at the White House, but Canada had been the star. Elizabeth, one journalist wrote, had not been prepared for "either the size, or the warmth or the vociferousness of her welcome".

Regrettably, one Canadian's advice had not been heeded: "Let's give the princess and her husband something they'll never forget... a trip with no speeches at all!" This was a lot to ask so the princess was doubtless a little hoarse when she set off home from Portugal Cove, Newfoundland.

The other major trip as princess was brought to a premature close. The plan was to visit Australia, New Zealand and South Africa, but she only got as far as Kenya. Just a few days into the journey, on 6 February 1952, Elizabeth returned from a break at Treetops Hotel to dreadful news from home: the king was dead.

President Truman provides Princess Elizabeth with a lift from Washington National Airport to the White House

should be cancelled: a notion that Whitehall immediately pooh-poohed. Similar tensions cast a pall over the stay in Uganda. The British governor had recently sent the pro-secession leader of Buganda (the largest traditional Ugandan kingdom) into exile - another example of British heavy-handedness - and, with matters still unresolved, a postponement of the Queen's visit was recommended. The request was, again, immediately dismissed, no major disturbances ensued, and the trip would be better remembered for her opening of the Owen Falls dam.

Mercifully, the preceding visit to Aden had been free from diplomatic anxiety. Though nothing much more than a glorified inspection of the troops, the few hours in Aden did possess a certain charm. One participant remembered a rather jumbled affair. "It was cool in the stands," he explained. "The parade marched on. The RAF did their best. The band of the Aden Protectorate Levies had turned out in green and white (no-one seemed to know why) and looked fine. There was a motley collection of other troops - Levies, Armed Police, Somaliland Scouts, Government Guards and Ingrams' Hadrami Legion wearing white frocks and, for the first time in their lives, sandals." On cue, the Queen and Prince Philip "were taken round the parade in a Land Rover. They looked as if they were going to fall off".

Malta, put on an excellent show. The islanders were pleased to see their most famous former resident but, at the last hurdle, everything became rather menacing in Gibraltar. The rival claims of Spain and Britain were very much in the headlines and General Franco took great pleasure in condemning the trip. The Spanish ambassador was sent with warnings of unavoidable protests to the British foreign secretary, Anthony Eden, who was flabbergasted by Spain's audacity.

Amid all this, Gibraltar's governor acted in extraordinarily

The final leg: the Queen and Prince Philip during their brief visit to Gibraltar

The Queen congratulates Aunty Tot after the horse's victory at the Brisbane race track

Home safe and sound. Britannia passes under Tower Bridge on 15 May 1954

"A TENNIS RACKET, A PAIR OF SHOES, AND THE SOUND OF RAISED VOICES FLEW OUT OF THE CHALET DOOR"

Queen Elizabeth during her flying visit to Aden, preparing to bestow knighthoods on Claude Pelly and Sayyid Abubakr

irresponsibly. Without seeking permission, he announced that Spanish people would be more than welcome to pop over the border during the Queen's visit: this at a time when the Spanish press was busily fomenting agitation and when there were genuine death threats against the Queen. The governor was reprimanded and, when the Queen arrived, the border was tightly controlled. The islanders went overboard in their expressions of fidelity and, as one newspaper put it, the 27,000 people, many of them servicemen, would probably "tear to pieces anyone discovered in their midst with evil designs, and that was sufficient guarantee of their Majesties' safety".

Looking back

The grandest of tours had certainly managed to combine moments of exuberance and boredom. It had been fun to watch a life-saving demonstration at Bondi Beach, visit the Ellerslie race track in New Zealand, or marvel at the Waitomo glowworm Cave. Who would not have enjoyed being presented with traditional Māori feather cloaks or having one's first taste of kava-root tea?

But it wasn't all smooth sailings. When a poliomyelitis health scare hit Western Australia, the prime minister insisted the royal party sleep on SS Gothic and eat nothing that hadn't been prepared on the ship. Just occasionally, tempers flared. During a weekend off, Elizabeth and Philip headed to the Yarra Ranges in Victoria, and the press came

along. All of a sudden, a tennis racket, a pair of shoes, and the sound of raised voices flew out of the chalet door. A minor domestic tiff was clearly underway but the royal press secretary sprang into action, demanding any photos of the incident be handed over. Within minutes, a smiling Queen was on deck. "I am sorry for that little interlude," she is supposed to have said, "but, as you know, it happens in every marriage."

The tour had been kind to the growing pile of sumptuous gifts. An organisation of the ladies of South Australia and Adelaide clubbed together for an opal necklace and earring set, which boasted 180 diamonds and the finest chunk of opal ever to emerge from the mine at Andamooka. The 'Women of Auckland' were not to be outdone and came up with a diamond and platinum brooch in the shape of a famous New Zealand emblem, the silver birch.

Frippery aside, however, the Queen was entitled to a sense of achievement when she made it back to Britain. Winston Churchill certainly thought so. Speaking in the Commons on 17 May 1954, he announced that "the gleaming episode of the Queen's journey among her peoples, their joy in welcoming her and the impact of her personality upon their vast numbers constitutes an event which stands forth without an equal in our records, and casts a light - clear, calm, gay and benignant - upon the whole human scene".

Churchill was laying it on a bit thick, as he was always apt to do in his rhetoric, but his sentiments found a receptive audience. Challenges lay ahead but, for a moment, it was not unreasonable to talk about a job well done or believe, as the Queen put it in her Christmas message later in the year, that the Commonwealth hearth had become more precious than ever before.

DESTINATIONS DURING THE COMMONWEALTH TOUR OF 1953-54

01 JAMAICA
25–27 NOV 1953

Here, leaders from other West Indies islands were given the opportunity to hold discussions with the Queen at Montego Bay. It was then off to a round of public engagements in Kingston, including an address to the joint legislative assembly.

02 BERMUDA
24–25 NOV 1953

First established as a British colony in 1607, Bermuda welcomed the royal couple at the capital, Hamilton. They arrived after an overnight flight on board the BOAC stratocruiser Canopus which had to make a detour or two to avoid stormy weather.

03 GIBRALTAR
10 MAY 1954

An enjoyable time was had by all, including Prince Charles and Princess Anne, who had joined the royal party at Malta. The children were particularly impressed by the rock's famous apes. By 13 May, Britannia was dropping anchor off Cornwall for the night and, by 15 May, passing under Tower Bridge.

04 MALTA
3–7 MAY 1954

Following a stopover in Tobruk, the Queen was guaranteed a warm welcome on the Mediterranean island which had served as a part-time home during the early years of her marriage. The royal party departed on new floating digs: the Royal Yacht Britannia.

05 ADEN
27 APRIL 1954

Though little more than a brief meet-and-greet largely taking up with inspecting troops, the locals certainly remembered the day when Her Majesty came to town.

06 UGANDA
28–30 APRIL 1954

Another destination where misgivings over the interventionist nature of British rule threatened to overshadow the celebrations. As it turned out, the visit was free of major incidents though the schedule was slightly rejigged. The royal couple left Entebbe, as they had arrived in the country, by air.

07 CEYLON
10–21 APRIL 1954

Perhaps no destination did a better job of combining lighthearted outings and the spectre of tough decisions about Britain's future role in local politics. Along the way, a new university was formally launched, ancient Buddhist temples were visited, and a session of parliament was opened.

08 THE COCOS ISLANDS
5 APRIL

An odd choice for the itinerary, this was nonetheless the first port of call on the trip back to Europe. After 90 minutes, mostly taken up by a garden party and the replenishing of supplies, the Queen embarked for Ceylon.

09 AUSTRALIA
3 FEBRUARY – 1 APRIL 1954

The tour's longest visit. The country was warming up for impassioned debate over its future relationship with Britain, but the Queen's travels, which took in every part of the nation with the exception of the Northern Territory, was a huge success.

10 NEW ZEALAND
23 DECEMBER 1953 – 30 JANUARY 1954

One of the longest and most wide-ranging stretches of the tour. Elizabeth was the first reigning British monarch to visit the country and the crowds responded with appropriate enthusiasm to a dizzying schedule, involving both north and south islands.

11 FIJI
17–19 DEC 1953

A lengthy voyage on the SS Gothic, including passage through the Panama Canal, came to an end with the Queen's arrival at Suva. Though only here for a short visit, the Queen and Prince Philip were able to enjoy one of the most relaxed periods of their tour. A lengthy voyage on the SS Gothic, including passage through the Panama Canal, came to an end with the Queen's arrival at Suva. Though only here for a short visit, the Queen and Prince Philip were able to enjoy one of the most relaxed periods of their tour.

12 TONGA
19–20 DEC 1953

A trip by flying boat brought the royals to Tonga. Just 24 hours on the island still allowed the Queen to be reacquainted with the charismatic Queen Salote.

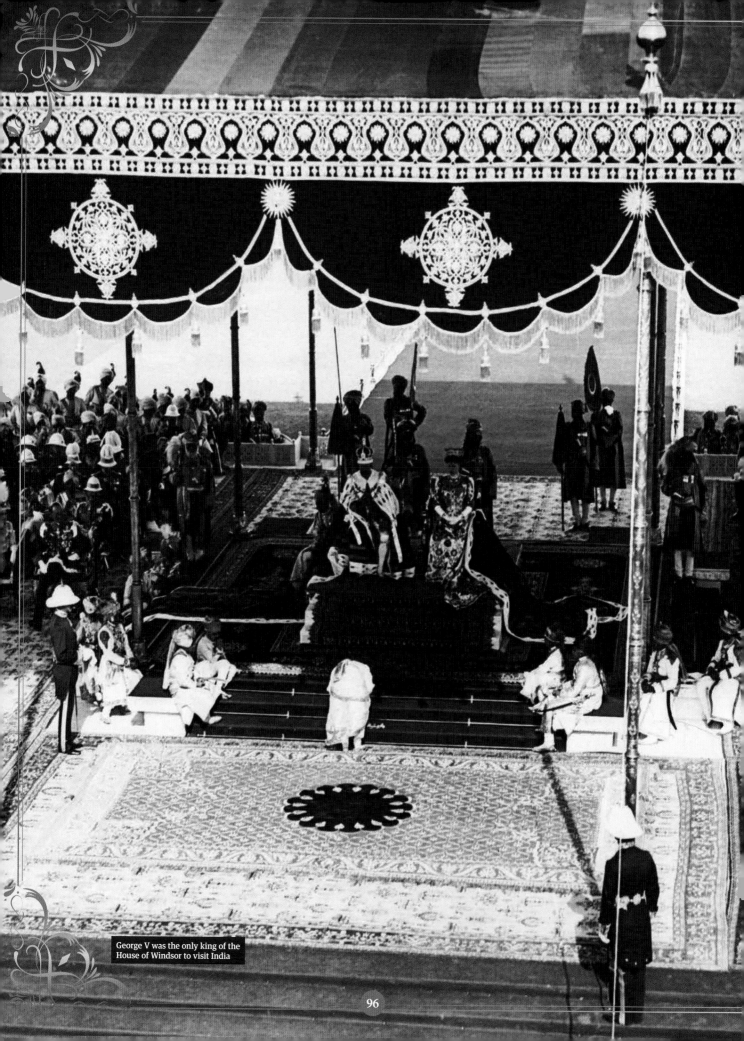

George V was the only king of the
House of Windsor to visit India

END OF EMPIRE, BIRTH OF COMMONWEALTH

The Windsors inherited an empire on which the sun never set, but they have watched it fade to be replaced by a Commonwealth that is valued by them and its members

The Windsors briefly ruled the biggest empire any British royal House had known, but in the course of less than a century they watched it disappear. However, the loss of a dominion on which the sun never set made way for the creation of a Commonwealth of Nations, which has set its own standards in international relations.

When the House of Windsor came into being in July 1917, Britain still ruled the vast British Empire. It incorporated around one-quarter of the world's population and included Australia, Canada, New Zealand, India, Nigeria, South Africa and Burma. Actual power in different parts of the empire varied enormously by 1917, with Canada, Newfoundland, New Zealand and Australia as well as the Union of South Africa having taken on the self-governing status of dominions. But where British rule was tighter, anger was beginning to bubble up, as in India, and even spill over into rebellion against the imperial system, as it had done in Ireland.

The importance placed on empire was also shown in 1917 when the prime minister, David Lloyd George, invited the leaders from the Dominions to join the Imperial War Cabinet. In the same year, George V created a new system of honours to reward those who had assisted Britain during the war in noncombatant roles. The Most Excellent Order of the British Empire introduced many of the honours we know today and took as its motto 'For God and Empire'.

However, World War I had already shown the cracks in the imperial structure. Britain had declared war on Germany on its own behalf and that of its empire, and all the countries under its control sent soldiers to fight in the conflict. Around 2.5 million took part in the Great War, the largest number coming from India. When peace finally came, the Treaty of Versailles increased the spread of the British Empire with Palestine, Trandjordan, Iraq, Tanganyika, Togoland and parts of Cameroon added. An additional 13 million people came under the nominal rule of the House of Windsor, while its territorial hold now covered around one-fifth of the world's land mass.

But the discussions that followed World War I also showed the rapid changes engulfing the empire as the dominions signed their own peace treaties. Meanwhile, the 1916 Easter Uprising in Ireland and the subsequent civil war there had made independence a pressing issue. In fact, the societal changes brought by World War I focused minds on demands for more self-determination across the empire.

None of this was lost on George V, who took a close interest in his territories. At the start of his reign, he had headed to India for the Delhi Durbar, which presented him to the country as its emperor, but his involvement was much more than ceremonial. He followed political developments closely and was alarmed by some parts of the British government policy against the continued unrest in Ireland.

In 1921, he accepted an invitation to open the new parliament in Belfast where he appealed for conciliation between the warring factions and then watched with satisfaction as a truce was agreed soon afterwards leading to the signing of the Anglo-Irish Treaty at the end of the year. A royal proclamation led to the Irish Free State Constitution Act of 1922, the separation of Northern Ireland and self dominion for the new Irish Free State.

But while King George consulted politicians about the state of his realms, he was less enthusiastic about touring them. He often said he would visit all of them or none at all, and with plenty to occupy him at home, it was his family, and particularly his two eldest sons, who became busy touring the many lands that came under royal rule.

The early years of the Windsors saw the House's younger members take on an increasing number of tours to the empire. Edward, then Prince of Wales, visited Canada in 1919 and Australia the following year, ensuring a visible presence for the dynasty in its dominions. In 1924, the newly married duke and duchess of York headed off on an extensive tour of British colonies in eastern Africa. In 1927, they spent six months in Australia and New Zealand. These tours were designed to give a visible presence of the 'mother country' in the lands that still nominally belonged to her.

THE LAST DAY OF THE EMPIRE

The Prince of Wales was a witness to the end of the imperial realms once ruled by the Windsors

In the dark, final hours of 30 June 1997, the British Empire came to its ultimate end. Just before midnight, the Prince of Wales stood up to read a message from the Queen, just minutes before Britain formally handed Hong Kong over to China. As midnight approached, the National Anthem was played and the Union Flag was lowered, bringing down the final curtain on an imperial structure that had, at one point, defined the rule of the House of Windsor.

Hong Kong had become part of the empire during the reign of Queen Victoria and negotiations about handing it over to China had been going on for decades by the time the official transfer of power took place. Prince Charles wrote at the time that some of the events, including one performance by the Hong Kong Police Force to mark the transition, were so moving that there were "very few dry eyes in the house".

The prince looked emotional, too, as midnight struck. The first moments of 1 July 1997 saw the Chinese flag raised over Hong Kong as it became part of different country. And the Prince of Wales walked away from the ceremony soon afterwards, having handed over the final part of an empire that he himself was never destined to rule.

Prince Charles takes a final salute as Hong Kong passes from Britain to China in 1997

The importance of empire was also stressed at home in the years after World War I. In 1919, the Prince of Wales became president of the Organising Committee of the British Empire Exhibition, which was designed to promote links and boost trade between countries. That exhibition, which eventually took place at Wembley between 23 April 1924 and 31 October 1925, involved 56 of the 58 imperial territories and became a physical display of the almost unimaginable extent of the empire. Each country had a pavilion that reflected its own culture while halls housing industrial, technological and historical displays were also included in the mini empire that took over Wembley. The royal family were frequent visitors and, in total, 17 million people visited the exhibition. But it was to prove a final curtain call rather than a launch pad for a new version of empire.

Just a year later, the seventh Imperial Conference was held in London, bringing together the prime ministers and leading politicians of the dominions. On the table were demands for complete autonomy. The countries had already won the right to set their own foreign policy at the conference of 1923, but the 1926 meeting produced the Balfour Declaration, which stated, for the first time, that the dominions were to be "autonomous communities... equal in status" – in other words, no longer subordinate to Britain. Those present decided the dominions would form a "Commonwealth of Nations".

It was a move that George V openly welcomed but privately mourned. In 1928, the then-colonial secretary, Leo Amery, recalled lunching with the king where George had expressed, more than once, his unhappiness with the constitutional changes taking place. When the Statute of Westminster gave full legal standing to the 1926 alterations in 1931, the king was equally disgruntled. He believed, although never stated publicly, that the documents had been drawn up to keep just a few of the dominions happy.

The Statute of Westminster meant that, from 1931 onwards, Britain had no control over the laws of those dominions and their parliaments could dispense with British legislation they disagreed with. Meanwhile, the Irish Free State issued a new constitution in 1937 that further distanced it from British rule, and it marked one of the final steps on the road to the declaration of a fully independent republic.

The change in status was reflected in one of the most important ceremonies the House of Windsor had known. In May 1937, King George VI was crowned, putting a final end to the turbulence caused by the abdication of his brother, Edward VIII, in December 1936. However, his coronation oath had to be changed to reflect the new, autonomous status of the dominions. The changes were further underlined in 1939 when Britain took up arms against Nazi Germany. This time, the dominions made their own declarations of war and the Irish Free State chose to stay neutral.

World War II was George VI's finest hour, but while his personal courage and role in rallying support for the fight against Nazism even in the darkest days of the conflict became one of the most enduring legacies of the House of Windsor, the same conflict also saw new pressures brought to bear on the empire that would ultimately lead to its fragmentation. Colonies including Singapore, Burma, Malaya and Hong Kong were occupied by Japanese forces, who had joined the war on the side of Hitler, while Australia and New Zealand relied heavily on the United States during parts of the conflict, leading to new alliances.

The king often broadcast across the world, on Empire Day, to rally troops and spirits, and he had visited Malta during his stay with Allied troops in northern Africa. His contribution won continuing admiration, but once victory was secured and the occupied colonies set free, a new demand for self-rule began to take hold in many parts of the British Empire.

The demise of the imperial structure was one that George VI had long been aware of. At the start of the war, writing to the US ambassador to London, Joseph Kennedy, the king had acknowledged that some were already speaking of a "loss of prestige of the British Empire", but he still believed in the links that bound its nations together, adding: "The British Empire has once again shown to the World a united front." However, almost as soon as the war was over, that united front began to melt away.

The demands for independence now being made around the empire found support in the newly elected Labour government that was led to power in 1945 by Clement Atlee. They were

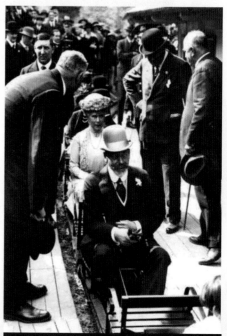

King George V and Queen Mary were regular visitors to the British Empire Exhibition, which dominated London in 1924 and 1925

The Queen and the duke of Edinburgh on
their Commonwealth tour of India in 1961

©Getty

"HIS CORONATION OATH HAD TO BE CHANGED TO REFLECT THE NEW, AUTONOMOUS STATUS OF THE DOMINIONS"

most pressing in India, where a campaign for self-determination and ultimately complete autonomy had been continuing for decades.

In 1942, Mahatma Gandhi and the Indian National Congress had come close to forcing Britain out of the country, and Winston Churchill had struck a deal, promising them independence after the war if they would keep supporting the empire while the conflict continued to rage. That move had surprised and angered George VI, but by 1947, he had finally realised that this unwanted change was inevitable.

The king became increasingly concerned about the possibility of conflict in India itself and, when the government recalled Lord Wavell as viceroy of India, George insisted he be replaced with his cousin Lord Louis Mountbatten, who was committed to introducing independence as quickly as possible. The Indian National Congress was now able to call the shots and the economic damages of war, as well as a prevailing sense of change, meant that Britain was in no position to fight.

The king insisted Mountbatten be given clear instructions, but events over took both of them

and soon after his arrival in India in March 1947, Lord Louis realised that swift actions were needed. Working with Jawaharlal Nehru, leader of the Indian National Congress, he drew up a plan for partition as the threat of conflict intensified. India became independent on 15 August 1947, the same day that the new, self-governing country of Pakistan came into being.

Within a year, Burma and Ceylon had also broken away from the empire, while 1948 saw Britain withdraw from Palestine, which was now left in the hands of the United Nations. In 1949, the Irish Free State formally became the Republic of Ireland. George VI, meanwhile, took advice on what he should now call himself as he had reigned, since 1936, as 'Rex Imperator'. In the end, he chose to sign his name as 'George R'.

The king also took on a new role as 'head of the Commonwealth'. The organisation had started to take shape following the

The duke and duchess of York visited Katoomba, Australia, in 1927 as part of their worldwide tour

Balfour Declaration of 1926, but when the new Indian government decided it would declare the country a republic, questions were asked over how that would affect the Commonwealth that was officially led by the king.

The decision of Indian politicians to recognise George VI as "the symbol of the free association" of the members of the Commonwealth led to the London Declaration of 1949, which described its countries as "free and equal members" with the aim of "freely co-operating in the pursuit of peace liberty and progress". It was the start of a new union, but yet another death knell for the dying empire.

The floral emblems of all the nations of the Commonwealth were embroidered onto the veil worn by Meghan Markle at her wedding on 19 May 2018

"THE DUCHESS OF SUSSEX LATER CHOSE TO DECORATE HER WEDDING VEIL WITH THE EMBLEMS OF THE COMMONWEALTH COUNTRIES"

The early years of Elizabeth II's reign were marked by a rapid wave of change across the imperial structure once ruled by the Windsors. In her Christmas Day broadcast of 1953, the Queen spoke of the Commonwealth as an "entirely new conception, built on... friendship, loyalty and the desire for freedom and peace". One of her first acts following her coronation was to embark on a major tour, taking her to the countries of the Commonwealth and the empire. But as the Queen and the duke of Edinburgh greeted cheering crowds in Australia, Canada and Jamaica, more countries were declaring independence. Sudan was granted self-government in 1953 and became independent in 1956. The following year, Malaya broke away, while Africa's Gold Coast declared independence as Ghana.

Meanwhile, the Suez Crisis of 1956 had exposed Britain's limitations as a world power.

In 1960, Harold Macmillan made his famous "winds of change" speech in South Africa, a formal recognition of the evolving nature of the relationship between Britain and its empire. Within a decade, nearly all the remaining colonies in Africa had become independent of Britain. In the Caribbean, Jamaica and Trinidad and Tobago declared independence in 1962 with Barbados following in 1966, while Britain's last colony on the American mainland, Honduras, became self-governing in 1964.

In the decades that followed, most other territories followed suit. But while their moves to independence made headlines, the expected pattern was for countries to break away from an empire that was fading into history. There were problems. Turbulence in Rhodesia led to civil war and in 1979, British rule was briefly reimposed while an international settlement was arranged.

Meanwhile, independence in Kenya followed the Mau Mau uprising. When Rhodesia achieved independence as Zimbabwe in 1980, Britain lost its last African holding. The end of empire came with the handover of Hong Kong to China in 1997, following which 14 countries remain under the sovereignty of Britain and its head of state, the Queen. They were renamed the British Overseas Territories in 2002.

While the House of Windsor has, like many a royal dynasty before it, seen an empire disappear, its senior members have taken on an important role in building and developing the organisation that replaced it, the Commonwealth. The Queen made no secret of her devotion to the Commonwealth, for many years travelling to the heads of government meetings held around the world. She has also attended many of the Commonwealth Games, held every four years, and which grew from the Empire Games that were first set up in 1930.

When she succeeded her father in 1952, there were few questions as to whether she should also become head of the Commonwealth. However, in 2018 she publicly intervened in the debate as to whether the same role should pass to her son, the Prince of Wales, when he takes the throne. She gave her backing to Charles and the group's leaders followed suit, guaranteeing the House of Windsor a leading role in an organisation that it helped to establish.

And the Commonwealth clearly remains vital to the royal family. Just before Prince Harry married Meghan Markle in May 2018, the Queen appointed her grandson as a Commonwealth Youth Ambassador, a role that saw him promote links between young people and leaders to address social challenges around the world. Harry made it clear that his new wife would join him in the work while the official assent to their marriage was decorated with the Commonwealth emblem, underlining their commitment to the organisation. The duchess of Sussex later chose to decorate her wedding veil with the emblems of all the Commonwealth countries.

It was more than a superficial gesture. The starring role given to the Commonwealth at the royal wedding showed the continuing bond the House of Windsor has with the countries that it once ruled. Regular tours and visits to lands that were once part of the empire are a major part of the royal diary, while the Queen's interest in the welfare of the communities across the Commonwealth was often given public expression in her Christmas Day features strongly. While the nature of its relationship with its many countries may have changed, the bond the House of Windsor feels for its empire has never diminished.

Marlborough House was home to two Windsor matriarchs before becoming the headquarters of the Commonwealth

THE ROYAL HOME OF THE COMMONWEALTH

The 'granny house' of the Windsors is now the base for the organisation that covers half the world

The Commonwealth may be a modern institution, but its headquarters are in one of London's oldest and most regal buildings. The organisation is based at Marlborough House, built for a favourite of Queen Anne, and it's the place where two queen consorts retreated in widowhood.

Marlborough House, designed by Christopher Wren, was built in the 1700s for Sarah, Duchess of Marlborough, who at the time was still a confidante of Queen Anne. However, the two would part company in 1711, shortly after the house was completed. It was taken over by the Crown in 1817 and in the following years was home to a number of royals, becoming a favourite residence of Queen Victoria's eldest son, Edward, and his wife, Alexandra.

Alexandra set up home there in 1910 following the death of her husband, and her devoted son, King George V, often called on her there in the years leading up to her own death in 1925. In 1936, George's own widow, Queen Mary, chose Marlborough House as her own residence after departing Buckingham Palace.

The red-brick, Grade I-listed building is now the seat of the Commonwealth Secretariat, the main institution of the organisation. It is here that planning for the meetings takes place and where much of the Commonwealth's policies are developed and refined.

Lord Louis Mountbatten, the last viceroy, announces independence for India in 1947

The Queen allowed cameramen unprecedented access to her family's private life while they filmed *Royal Family* documentary. Here, they are being filmed having breakfast at Windsor Castle

AN ERA OF INSTABILITY

The 1960s and 1970s presented a time when both Queen and country faced a period of great change

Between 1964 and 1976, many social and cultural changes were taking place in Britain as the Swinging Sixties got underway, Beatlemania dominated the headlines and Harold Wilson led the first Labour government since the 1940s. It was an exciting and eventful time for everyone - including the royal family.

When Queen Elizabeth gave birth to her fourth and final child, Prince Edward, on 10 March 1964, she was absolutely delighted with her new baby. "Goodness, what fun it is to have a baby in the house again!" she exclaimed, clearly relishing the prospect of enjoying a more relaxed relationship with her two youngest children. When her eldest two children, Charles and Anne, were born, the Queen was in her early 20s and had not expected to inherit the throne for several more decades. By the time of Prince Edward's birth, however, much had changed: she was just a month shy of her 38th birthday and had been on the throne for over a decade.

Queen Elizabeth was no longer the shy and rather awkward young princess who had so disliked public displays of affection and felt as though her onerous royal duties struck a poor balance with her other duties as a wife and mother. Instead, she was now a confident, mature woman who was more than ready and able to rise to the challenge of being both a mother and a queen. However, although the Queen was happy

to have another baby, her duties quickly took her elsewhere. She agreed to go on a ten-day tour of Canada at the end of the year - it was a disaster, marred by an assassination threat, booing in Quebec City and a riot in Montréal, all of which challenged her famous calmness and sang-froid, and she no doubt wished that she had stayed at home instead.

Over the next decade, the royal family would see many other challenges as the world changed and the elder royal children matured and started their own independent lives, with plenty of mishaps and dramas along the way. It was also a period of great personal satisfaction for the Queen as she worked hard to boost the royal family's popularity. She made them more visible by authorising a groundbreaking documentary and also introducing walkabouts to her royal engagements, which allowed her to meet more members of the public.

She also enjoyed working with her first Labour prime minister, Harold Wilson, who was elected in October 1964 and stayed in power until June 1970, when he was ousted by the Conservative Edward Heath. Unlike the well-heeled privately educated men who had been her previous prime ministers, Wilson was of proudly provincial stock and had attended a grammar school before going to Oxford, where he excelled in Economics. If the Queen had felt nervous about dealing with a noted socialist, she need not have worried;

theybecame great friends and enjoyed their weekly meetings, which often went well over the allotted time as they had so much to talk about.

Within just a few weeks of Prince Edward's birth, the inner circle of the royal household was shaken by the revelation that the Surveyor of the Queen's Pictures, the eminent art historian Sir Anthony Blunt (who was a distant cousin of the Queen Mother), had confessed to acting as a Soviet spy. He had been recruited by Guy Burgess in the 1930s, and was in fact the hitherto mysterious 'Fourth Man' of the notorious Cambridge Spy Ring, made up of intellectual communists. Although there had been rumours about Blunt's involvement in espionage for several years, the revelation came as a huge shock to the Queen, who had no idea.

In exchange for his confession, Blunt was offered immunity from prosecution and for his secret to be embargoed for 15 years, which meant he was able to continue in his post as usual. However, after his secret was revealed in 1979, his life was effectively ruined. He was forced to resign his post in the royal household and was stripped of the knighthood that had been awarded to him in 1956. After he died of a heart attack in 1983, Blunt's memoirs revealed that he believed that becoming a spy had been "the biggest mistake" of his life.

A very different sort of drama was brewing elsewhere in the

The Queen was deeply moved, often to tears, by the sights that she saw when she visited Aberfan shortly after the disaster in October 1966

royal household as the marriage of the Queen's younger sister, Princess Margaret, to photographer Lord Snowdon became increasingly unhappy. The birth of the couple's second child, Sarah, in May 1964 brought them together for a time, but things quickly began to unravel against a vivid backdrop of glamorous celebrity parties, expensive overseas holidays and possible alcohol and drug abuse. While her elder sister felt distinctly uncomfortable in celebrity circles, Margaret loved to surround herself with artists, actors and musicians – The Beatles and The Rolling Stones dominated headlines at this time and she was happy to absorb them into her social circle.

Although her husband had been unfaithful throughout their marriage, Margaret reportedly did not have her first affair until around 1966 when she began a liaison with Anthony Barton, a friend of the Snowdons and godfather to their daughter. She had a number of discreet extra-marital affairs

"1966 WOULD BE A YEAR BOTH OF TRIUMPH AND TRAGEDY THAT UNITED THE NATION"

until she met Roderic 'Roddy' Llewellyn, who was 17 years her junior, in 1973. Although Margaret described their relationship as a "loving friendship", it's clear that she was devoted to him. When photos of the pair on holiday together appeared on the front page of *The News of the World*, it was the catalyst for the final breakdown and end of her marriage, which resulted in a divorce in July 1978. While Lord Snowdon swiftly married again, Margaret would remain unmarried for the rest of her life.

1966 would be a year both of triumph and tragedy that united the nation in celebration and mourning. Ever since England had been awarded hosting duties in 1960, excitement about the FIFA World Cup had been mounting. Although England

had hitherto failed to win the coveted Jules Rimet Trophy, it was hoped that a home crowd might give them an advantage at the 1966 tournament. The final against West Germany, which was held at Wembley Stadium on 30 July, was watched by 94,924 football fans in the stadium itself along with an astonishing 32.3 million at home. To this day, it remains the most watched television event ever in the UK. After being awarded the trophy by the Queen, England captain Bobby Moore lifted it over his head – the moment became one of the most iconic images of the 20th century.

The country was still in a state of elation after this unprecedented win in the autumn of 1966, until news broke on 21 October about the terrible tragedy that had befallen the small Welsh mining

The Aberfan disaster of 1966 shocked the nation

Among the trials and tribulations of the 1970s, there was still a cause for celebration. On 7 June 1977, over 1 million people lined London's streets to watch their monarch travel in the gilded state coach to St Paul's Cathedral to begin the festivities that would commemorate Elizabeth's 25 years on the throne. At the cathedral, 2,700 guests took part in the ceremony, while millions watched at home.

Street parties - the staple of national British celebrations - were held all over the country. The Queen also toured the nation and Commonwealth, visiting Western Samoa, New Zealand, Australia, India, Scotland, Wales, Northern Ireland, Canada and the Caribbean. Military tattoos were held across the territories, too, and a test cricket match between England and Australia was held at Lord's on 16 June.

The Silver Jubilee had more lasting effects, though, including the opening of the Piccadilly line on the London Underground on 16 December 1977 and the naming of the Silver Jubilee Walkway and the Jubilee Gardens in South Bank, London.

But not everyone joined in the festivities. British punk rock band the Sex Pistols released their song 'God Save the Queen' in 1977, a track with heavy anti-monarchist undertones. It reached No. 2 in the UK charts, and on 7 June 1977 the band tried to play it from a boat on the Thames. The song itself had been banned by the BBC, but despite that, it has been claimed that it should have reached No. 1 and that the charts had been fixed that week to stop it from reaching the top spot.

village of Aberfan. One of the enormous colliery spoil tips, precariously balanced on a hillside above the village, had collapsed and descended upon the village in a horrifying avalanche of slurry, almost completely burying Pantglas Junior School. There were 144 deaths, including those of 116 children, most of them pupils at the school.

Early the next morning, Lord Snowdon visited the site and spoke to parents of victims and rescue workers while his brother-in-law, the duke of Edinburgh, arrived a few hours later. However, the Queen did not visit until the following week, a delay that she would later describe as one of her biggest regrets as she felt that she should have gone there much sooner. She would ultimately visit the village four more times over the years, and the people of Aberfan still believe that her continued interest in them has done a great deal to help them recover from the disaster. It

reminded them that they had not been forgotten by the world.

The 1960s are remembered as an era of great social and cultural change. The younger generation, who had been born immediately after the war and now benefited from the new prosperity that had succeeded post-war austerity, celebrated all that was fresh, modern and innovative. In the eyes of many, the royal family epitomised the dull and old-fashioned past that they were trying to forget. It was time for the royals to reflect on their place in this new world and consider ways to make themselves appear more relevant and approachable.

In early 1968, the Queen decided to authorise a groundbreaking documentary about her family. Ostensibly it was to celebrate the investiture of Prince Charles as Prince of Wales the following year, but it would also make the family appear

The Queen greets wellwishers on her tour of the United Kingdom during her Silver Jubilee celebrations in 1977

Unlike her sister, Princess Margaret felt very much at home with celebrities and was clearly delighted to meet The Beatles at a film premiere in July 1964

Footballer Bobby Moore receives the Jules Rimet trophy from the Queen after beating West Germany in the 1966 World Cup final

more accessible and less remote. Over the next year, cameramen were allowed unprecedented access to the Queen and her family (with one notable absentee - Philip's mother, Alice, who had moved into Buckingham Palace in 1967) as they went about their daily business. The filmmakers accumulated 43 hours of footage, which was condensed into a 110-minute documentary, titled *Royal Family*.

However, when it was screened in June 1969, with more than 30 million curious British viewers tuning in, the response was decidedly muted. Many critics thought that presenting the Queen and her family as ordinary people destroyed some of the intrinsic mystique of royalty, and that in the long term it would do them more harm than good. It was therefore decided that the film should be shelved and never again be broadcast in public.

When Prince Charles's investiture, a Medieval modern spectacle devised by Lord Snowdon, took place a few weeks later, it too was marred by controversy. Although the majority of Welsh people were in favour of the ceremony, a significant proportion - many of whom were members of Welsh nationalist and republican groups - made their disapproval known and even threatened to disrupt the event at Caernarfon Castle. Even the news that Prince Charles had spent several months learning about Welsh culture and had even been studying the Welsh language for the event did little to improve matters, although in the end the ceremony passed without incident.

While the royal family were preparing for the investiture, preparations of a very different kind were underway elsewhere as NASA got ready for one of the most exciting and highly anticipated events of the 20th century - the first manned Moon landing. The royal family were among the 650 million viewers worldwide who watched Neil Armstrong and Buzz Aldrin descend from Apollo 11's lunar lander on 20 July 1969, becoming the first men to walk on the Moon. It was a thrilling moment, and perhaps few were quite so excited as the duke of Edinburgh, who was deeply interested in the possibilities of extraterrestrial life and UFOs, even keeping a map of alleged sightings on a wall in Buckingham Palace. To actually see men walking on the Moon would have been absolutely fascinating for a man with his interests.

Meanwhile, his wife was also enthralled by the mission and deeply impressed by the bravery of the astronauts. "I salute the skills and courage which have brought man to the Moon," she wrote to them. "May this endeavour increase the knowledge and well being of mankind."

Elizabeth and Prince Philip were both delighted to meet the Apollo 11 crew when they attended a reception at Buckingham Palace later that year. Afterwards, Armstrong and Aldrin commented on how amazingly well informed and interested about their programme the Queen had been.

Prince Charles's investiture as Prince of Wales caused some controversy amongst Welsh nationalists and republicans, but despite threats to disrupt the event it was considered a great success

When Princess Anne turned 20 in August 1970, it meant that both of the Queen's eldest children were now officially out of their teens. Prince Charles graduated from Cambridge that summer, then began training with the RAF before emulating his father and grandfather by enlisting in the Royal Navy. In 1971, shortly after beginning his training, he met vivacious socialite Camilla Shand, with whom he was immediately smitten. Although it would turn out that she was actually

Prince Charles met the vivacious Camilla Shand in 1971, but the couple split up when he started his RAF training and she married someone else

more interested in his sister Anne's ex-boyfriend, a dashing Household Cavalry officer called Andrew Parker-Bowles, whom Camilla would eventually marry.

While her brother was starting his career, Princess Anne was concentrating on her passion for equestrian sports. She won the European Eventing Championships in 1971, which led to her being voted BBC Sports Personality of the Year a few months later. After breaking up with Andrew Parker-Bowles, she started seeing another noted equestrian, Lieutenant Mark Phillips of the Queen's Dragoon Guards. The couple married on 14 November 1973, and it was the first royal wedding since that of Princess Margaret in 1960. The nation relished the opportunity to celebrate the nuptials, while 100 million viewers around the world watched the live broadcast of the wedding. Like Lord Snowdon, Phillips was offered an earldom by the Queen, but he turned the honour down as he wanted his future children to have as normal a life as possible.

However much the newly married couple clearly wanted to enjoy a private and ordinary existence, they were soon reminded just how difficult that would be. Within five months of their wedding, in March 1974 they only narrowly avoided being kidnapped while driving down the

Despite her initial reservations, the Queen and her first Labour prime minister, Harold Wilson, developed an excellent professional relationship and became good friends

Princess Anne married fellow equestrian Captain Mark Phillips in Westminster Abbey on 14 November 1973

Queen Elizabeth II with the Apollo 11 astronauts, Michael Collins, Neil Armstrong and Buzz Aldrin, when she met them at Buckingham Palace

"IT WAS TIME FOR THE ROYALS TO REFLECT ON THEIR PLACE IN THIS NEW WORLD"

Mall. The assailant, Ian Ball, had forced their car to stop then shot Anne's chauffeur and protection officer as well as a journalist who attempted to intervene before demanding that the princess get out of her car. "Not bloody likely!" Anne retorted before making her escape. Ball then shot a police officer before finally being overpowered and arrested. The incident shocked the nation but luckily all those who were shot by Ball recovered from their injuries, while Princess Anne's calm composure and bravery were much admired and won her many new fans.

While Princess Anne's wedding in 1973 was the great royal celebration of the decade, there had been another much sadder event in June of the previous year when the Queen's uncle, the duke of Windsor, formerly King Edward VIII, was quietly laid to rest in the Royal Burial Ground at Frogmore House after lying in state in St George's Chapel at Windsor Castle. The duke, whose health had been failing for a number of years, had died in Paris on 28 May, just ten days after the Queen had paid

him a private visit while on a state visit to the French capital.

The duchess of Windsor accompanied her husband's body to England and stayed at Buckingham Palace, where it was noted that the Queen treated her with great kindness, probably prompted by the fact that the frail duchess was confused and disorientated and eventually had to be sedated on the day of the funeral. The Queen, as one observer noted later, "showed a motherly and nanny-like tenderness and kept putting her hand on the duchess's arm and glove".

Edward's abdication and subsequent behaviour over the years had done much to alienate him from his family as well as make him deeply unpopular with the British populace, but by the early 1970s it was clear that the Queen at least was ready to put it all firmly behind her. The duchess of Windsor developed dementia and lived as a virtual recluse for the last years of her life. When she died in April 1986, she was also accorded a funeral in St George's Chapel and then,

in the presence of the Queen and duke of Edinburgh as well as other members of the royal family, buried beside her husband.

Politics aside, the Queen was no doubt pleased when Harold Wilson was returned to power in March 1974. She had established a remarkable rapport and genuine friendship with the prime minister, and the pair were able to resume the weekly meetings that she had enjoyed so much. However, despite all of his socialist government's achievements when it came to making Britain a healthier, safer and fairer place to live, his period in office was a deeply stressful one. He dealt with the decolonisation of the former empire and, closer to home, the increasing threat of militant groups in Northern Ireland.

In March 1976, Wilson announced his resignation. As a mark of her respect, the Queen marked his departure by attending a dinner at 10 Downing Street - an honour that had only once before been accorded, to Winston Churchill. Although the Queen was sorry to lose Wilson, she also enjoyed dealing with his successor James Callaghan, who would remain in power until he was replaced in 1979 by Margaret Thatcher - which began an altogether different relationship between the Queen and her prime minister.

Images © Getty

A DECADE OF TRIUMPH AND TURBULENCE

The Queen lived through personal highs and lows in the 1980s, when the image of the monarchy and popular attitudes to the royals changed forever

Words **June Woolerton**

On a hot July day in 1982, the Queen led her family into St Paul's Cathedral in London for a service marking the end of a war that had claimed over 250 British lives. Just a year earlier, they had stood in the same church for a glittering royal wedding watched by hundreds of millions of people around the world. That mix of deep emotions, of celebration and commemoration, would mark the decade ahead. For Elizabeth II, the 1980s were a time of triumph and turbulence.

The famous marriage that had started the decade for the Windsors would come to dominate it. The Queen had been thrilled when her eldest son and heir to the throne, Prince Charles, had announced his engagement to Lady Diana Spencer in February 1981. The bride came from a family with long-standing links to the Windsors, but within moments of being introduced to the press as a princess-in-waiting, Diana had shown a star quality that brought legions of new fans to the royal family. By the time of her wedding, on 29 July 1981, she was a global superstar, while the apparent fairytale romance

she enjoyed with her handsome prince captivated endless imaginations. When the couple confirmed they were expecting a baby just months after the wedding, the direct succession was secured, with Elizabeth II now certain her line would continue to rule well into the 21st century.

Diana's arrival also underlined a change to the Queen's public image. While the monarch remained the centre of the House of Windsor, media and public interest in the 1980s focused on its younger members. The new Princess of Wales saw her fame grow rapidly, while the arrival of her two sons, William and Harry, in 1982 and 1984 provided a revamped version of the royal family that grabbed headlines. The Queen's role was seen as focused on state and constitutional matters, and she rarely attracted as much attention as Diana.

As the 1980s began, Elizabeth II was approaching the 30th anniversary of her accession. At the start of her reign politicians had worried about her ability to take on the responsibilities of her role, but three decades on the Queen was a respected stateswoman whose advice and counsel was sought after by those elected to govern throughout the world.

Margaret Thatcher, who had swept the Conservatives into government in 1979, made no secret of the high regard in which she held the monarchy. However, the relationship between the two women, which developed throughout the decade until Mrs Thatcher was forced from power in 1990, was sometimes fraught, although it always remained respectful. Their weekly audiences were vital as major issues engulfed the UK through the decade. Through the high unemployment of the early 1980s to the privatisation policies that accelerated following Thatcher's landslide election win in 1983 to riots over the Poll Tax as the 1990s began, the Queen was kept informed by her prime minister while exercising her own right to offer advice, which was always kept secret.

However, that bond of silence appeared to be threatened in 1986 when the *Sunday Times* published a story claiming the Queen found her prime minister "uncaring". It appeared in the aftermath of the miners' strike and was taken by some to be an indication that Elizabeth II had been disturbed by the social division in the areas affected. But it also

© Getty

The Queen's image was transformed into that of a doting grandmother as she saw her family expand in the 1980s

The Queen celebrated a special anniversary for 10 Downing Street with six of her prime ministers in 1985

The Queen's calm public image remained unruffled through the highs and lows of the 1980s

came at a time when the two women were known to hold different attitudes to dealing with the Apartheid regime in South Africa. Mrs Thatcher, at the time, opposed the ideas of sanctions, preferring to negotiate. The Queen was alarmed at the impact a lack of direct action could have on the Commonwealth. While neither side ever fully addressed the *Sunday Times* article, it only served to fuel rumours - later denied by Margaret Thatcher - that the two were far from friends.

The women had certainly become close during one of the biggest crises of the 1980s. When Argentina suddenly occupied the Falkland Islands on 2 April 1982, Mrs Thatcher immediately dispatched troops to counter the invasion. Among those listed to serve was Prince Andrew, second son of the Queen and the duke of Edinburgh. Elizabeth II dealt with the details of the conflict behind the scenes, but in public she was seen as the parent of a serving officer.

When the Falklands War ended after ten weeks, with the loss of 255 British personnel, it was Margaret Thatcher who took the salute at the London Victory Parade while the Queen led tributes at a service of commemoration at St Paul's Cathedral on 26 July 1982. But it was her appearance on the quayside in Portsmouth to welcome back her son that caught the imagination. Elizabeth II, as monarch and mother, became an iconic image of the decade.

Foreign politics also dominated in the 1980s. There was more friction between the Queen

The Queen's joy at her children's weddings in the 1980s was clear despite the pomp and ceremony of the days

and Mrs Thatcher when, in 1983, US forces landed in Grenada without informing the British government first. Elizabeth II was furious to see a Commonwealth country invaded and angrily ordered her prime minister to Buckingham Palace, forcing her to leave a cabinet meeting.

The incident, which ended just months later with the withdrawal of US troops, cast a shadow on

the strong relationship that the Queen developed with President Ronald Reagan during the decade. Elizabeth II had entertained the US leader at Windsor Castle in 1982 before enjoying a stay at his ranch in California the following year. The two got on famously well, and when the president left office in 1989 after serving two terms, the Queen made him an Honorary Knight Grand Cross of the Order of Bath.

The decade also saw Elizabeth II travel extensively to support ties between Britain and countries around the world. She made 17 state visits to countries, with five taking place in 1980 alone. Among her trips was a groundbreaking stay in China in 1986. The Queen also hosted another 20 state visits as world leaders made their way to

"THATCHER DISPATCHED TROOPS TO COUNTER THE INVASION. AMONG THOSE LISTED TO SERVE WAS PRINCE ANDREW"

The Queen, on her horse Burmese, during the 1981 Trooping the Colour parade during which she was shot at in an assassination attempt

MOTHER STILL KNOWS BEST
The Queen Mother remained an influential royal in private and in public

Fergie and Diana's relaxed and sometimes mischievous public image caused concern in royal circles

As the personal lives of her children began to make headlines in the 1980s, the Queen had one relative she knew she could rely on: her mother. Queen Elizabeth, the Queen Mother, had carved out a public role of genteel grandmother since the accession of her elder daughter. But behind palace walls she remained a steely source of strength in increasingly difficult times. She also provided some much-needed good publicity for the royal family. Throughout the decade, the Queen Mother continued a packed diary of royal engagements as well as several major overseas tours, including a string of visits to Canada.

There were nationwide celebrations for her 80th birthday as the decade got underway, while her appearance at the gates of her London home, Clarence House, for her special day every August became a popular royal tradition that pulled in ever-increasing crowds. Her charm and good humour were also invaluable weapons in the battle to keep public opinion on side. She was treated in hospital in 1982 and 1986 when fish bones became stuck in her throat but happily joked after one incident that the salmon had taken revenge on this keen royal fisher.

The Queen relied heavily on the support of her mother and sister as the 1980s became increasingly volatile for the royal family

London. At the start of the decade she had been kept waiting by the king of Morocco during her state visit to his country. By 1990, as one of the most experienced heads of state in the world, she was invited to make a historic trip to the newly unified Germany within months of the fall of the Berlin Wall.

The Queen had never made any secret of the huge importance she placed on the Commonwealth, and her devotion to it continued throughout the 1980s. She attended many of the heads of government meetings and took an interest in its changing membership as new nations, including Vanuatu and Saint Kitts and Nevis, took their place at the table. But her involvement went far deeper than photo calls. Decades later, a former prime minister of Canada, Brian Mulroney, would praise the Queen for her work in the Commonwealth during the 1980s, saying she had been instrumental behind the scenes in ensuring an end to Apartheid in South Africa.

It was during a visit to another Commonwealth nation, New Zealand, that the Queen faced one of several attacks in a decade where security and terror threats came to dominate. While touring Dunedin in 1981, a teenager fired a shot at her, missing. Details of the incident were kept secret for almost 30 years.

Just months earlier, another, very well-documented, assassination attempt had taken place in London. The Queen, riding her favourite horse, Burmese, was leading the annual Trooping the Colour parade in the capital when six blank shots rang out across the Mall. Burmese was spooked but Elizabeth II calmly brought her mount under control and maintained her composure as a security operation swung into place. 17-year-old Marcus Sarjeant was arrested and later admitted his motivation had been fame. He served three years in prison after being convicted under the Treason Act.

Just a year later, the Queen faced another threat when she awoke to find a 31-year-old man in her bedroom attempting to pull open the curtains. Michael Fagan had made his way into Buckingham Palace, stealing an ashtray as he stalked through its corridors before breaking it, leaving his hand covered in blood. A schizophrenic, as Fagan perched on the end of the Queen's bed he began to talk to her about his problems. Elizabeth II rang for help but received no response, pressing her emergency bell again before

The birth of Prince William in the summer of 1982 guaranteed the direct line of succession

By 1991 the Queen was aware the royal family was looking to a future filled with increased scrutiny

Princess Anne, created Princess Royal by the Queen in 1987, was one of the busiest members of the family as well as a great support to her

negotiating him to the door apparently to find him a drink. He was taken away soon afterwards. No criminal charges were pressed and Fagan received psychiatric support. Security around the Queen was immediately tightened following public outrage over the ease with which the palace had been breached.

The duke of Edinburgh had been absent at the time of the break in, but it was a rare gap in their diaries as Prince Philip remained a constant support to his wife. He was at her side as crowds gathered in the Mall in 1986 to celebrate her 60th birthday, and a year later they marked their 40th wedding anniversary.

The decade also saw them enter a new phase in their family lives. Five years after Charles and Diana's wedding, Prince Andrew married Sarah Ferguson at Westminster Abbey in another huge event that drew massive TV audiences. It was another good news story for the Windsors, while the Queen showed her approval of the union by making her second son the duke of York.

The arrival of two York princesses, Beatrice and Eugenie, in 1988 and 1990, provided more positive PR and saw the Queen's image transformed into that of a doting grandmother. She welcomed five of her eight grandchildren in the 1980s, and slowly the formal portraits that had characterised her reign were replaced by family photos of Elizabeth

and Philip enjoying time with the next generation of British royals.

But the Windsors were also developing a new, more glamorous image thanks to the huge interest shown in the duchess of York and the Princess of Wales. The Queen was reportedly irked by the way press interest in her daughters-in-law sometimes overshadowed more important royal duties, but she realised, sooner than anyone else, that it was part of the monarchy's evolution. Throughout the 1980s royal fashion became more of a talking point than ever before as Diana's style statements made headlines while Fergie's attempts to follow suit were judged, sometimes unkindly, to be failures.

However, this media interest brought a new set of problems for the Queen as the personal lives of her children began to make headlines. Elizabeth II had been raised in an age where the press was reverential and well remembered how news of the relationship between her uncle, Edward VIII, and

Rumours of a rift between the Prince and Princess of Wales gathered momentum in the late 1980s

THE QUEEN'S MOST SIGNIFICANT STATE VISIT

Political wrangling and undiplomatic comments from her consort didn't stop Elizabeth II turning a trip to China into a triumph

It became one of the most important tours the Queen ever undertook, but her state visit to China in October 1986 began against a backdrop of political wrangling. Elizabeth arrived in Beijing in the wake of difficult discussions between politicians there and in London over the return of Hong Kong to China when the British lease ran out in 1997.

However, the Queen's diplomacy throughout the visit was praised even if comments by the duke of Edinburgh led to one newspaper labelling him "the Great Wally of China". The couple had been photographed at the famous wall during the visit. The image of Elizabeth II and the duke of Edinburgh at the landmark became symbolic of a state visit that helped improve relations between Britain and China.

Equally impressive were the photos of the Queen and Prince Philip wandering among the famous terracotta warriors in Xi'an. The couple put on a show of their own when they entertained their hosts with a glittering banquet on board the royal yacht, Britannia. The first-ever state visit to China by a British monarch was judged a success and remains one of the most significant moments of her long reign.

The visit of the Queen and the duke of Edinburgh to the Great Wall of China in October 1986 remains an iconic moment in her reign

Wallis Simpson had remained secret until just days before the abdication. Now the royals were seen as fair game, and the Queen had to develop a new strategy for dealing with the press.

It wasn't easy. In 1987, the decision of her youngest son, Prince Edward, to leave the Royal Marines without completing his training drew criticism, as did his new TV programme, *It's a Royal Knockout*, which saw him joined by Princess Anne and the duke and duchess of York to lead teams competing for charity in a one-off show aired from the lawns at Alton Towers.

Media attention began to switch to younger members of the royal family in the 1980s, but the Queen remained at the heart of the monarchy

More difficult to deal with was ongoing speculation about the marriages of her children. As early as 1987 reports began to circulate of difficulties between Charles and Diana, while Anne announced her separation from Captain Mark Phillips in 1989 after persistent reports that the pair were unhappy and even involved in relationships with other people.

By the time the 1980s came to an end, front-page stories about the younger royals were a regular occurrence. The House of Windsor saw its popularity begin to decline. The Queen, meanwhile, was also dealing with the political upheaval caused by Mrs Thatcher's fall from power. Soon after John Major replaced her in Downing Street, UK troops were called into action in the Gulf War. In the aftermath of that conflict, Elizabeth II became the first British monarch to address the US Congress, praising the co-operation and mutual respect that existed between the two countries.

The speech was widely celebrated and grabbed some rare positive press attention for the Royal Family. As 1991 wore on, Charles and Diana's marriage was very openly unravelling, while rumours that the Duke and Duchess of York were close to parting gained momentum. The Queen's triumph in Washington was soon replaced on the front pages by the unrest in her family's private lives. It was an indicator of much harder times to come.

"NOW THE ROYALS WERE SEEN AS FAIR GAME, AND THE QUEEN HAD TO DEVELOP A NEW STRATEGY FOR DEALING WITH THE PRESS"

ELIZABETH'S ANNUS HORRIBILIS

Separations, divorces, fires, scandalous photos in the tabloids, and embarrassing, best-selling books... 1992 didn't shape up to be the best year

Words **Jon Wright**

The haunting image of Windsor Castle during the November 1992 fire

The aftermath of the Windsor fire: St George's Hall in terrible condition

Sarah Ferguson and her children leaving Balmoral under a cloud in August 1992

I t all began in a private chapel in the northeast wing. A spotlight had managed to ignite a curtain and, before too long, the flames were rampaging through some of Windsor Castle's most famous state rooms and apartments. St George's Hall, the state dining room, the grand reception room, and the red, green and white drawing rooms all took heavy damage. 15 hours were required to bring the fire under control and the resulting sight could only provoke shock and sadness: the blaze had found its way into more than 100 rooms, covering 7,000 square feet. 20 November had been a terrible day.

Mercifully, the losses of art and furniture had been minimal. The only significant casualties were a rosewood sideboard (reputedly by Pugin) and a mighty canvas depicting George III as he inspected the troops. If the flames had reached the Royal Library and Print Room, matters could have been much worse, although, almost as soon as the fire began, members of the household had managed to rescue the most precious books and drawings.

Lady Palmer, wife of the constable of the castle, remembered "an amazing sight - this line of people passing three or four books at a time - the Dean, to an electrician, to the elderly wife of a Military Knight, to a Keeper... to a Gurkha... to a Lay Clerk, to a painter... to a Minor Canon, to one of the girls who works in the shop". Similar salvage operations were mounted throughout the castle, often overseen by Prince Andrew, who had been on site at around 11.30am when the fire was first detected.

Just a few days later, on 24 November, the Queen gave a scheduled speech at London's Guildhall. She was still hoarse from a cold she had acquired while watching events unfold at the castle. The fire was only the latest blow in what the Queen described as an annus horribilis, and the press,

The Queen delivers the famous annus horribilis speech at the Guildhall

who had so readily pounced on the succession of earlier familial gaffes and missteps, came in for a bashing. Perhaps, the speech suggested, "history will take a slightly more moderate view than that of some contemporary commentators". Though what could one expect from "those whose task it is in life to offer instant opinions on all things great and small"? There was more than an ounce or two of petulance in such remarks, but the Queen also realised, and regretted, that many of her family's wounds had been self-inflicted.

The royalty's reputation was rooted in dignity and it had simply not measured up. "There can be no doubt, of course, that criticism is good for

people and institutions that are part of public life." Scrutiny, of a constructive kind, could be "an effective engine for change" and change was sorely needed. The marital antics of the Queen's children, one of the constant themes of the terrible year, might have been a good place to start.

A YEAR OF UNCOUPLINGS
The duke and duchess of York got the ball rolling. Their marriage had been in trouble for some time. She was tired of seeing so little of her husband (perhaps 40 days a year) because of his naval duties; he was tired of rumours surrounding his wife's private life. Over Christmas 1991, the couple had informed the Queen of their plans to separate and agreed to wait six months before making an announcement.

Unfortunately, the new year brought tabloid photos of Sarah living it up with the deep-pocketed Texan Steve Wyatt in Morocco. Incensed, Andrew brought matters to a

"AS SOON AS THE FIRE BEGAN, MEMBERS OF THE HOUSEHOLD HAD MANAGED TO RESCUE THE MOST PRECIOUS BOOKS AND DRAWINGS"

AND IN THE QUEEN'S CORNER...

Elizabeth II welcomed as much advice as possible during 1992. She found an ally in the prime minister, whose behind-the-scenes support was a godsend

John Major - as we were told endlessly at the time - was a 'different' kind of Conservative prime minister. This was code for the fact that he had started out as a lowly Brixton-based insurance clerk and hadn't received an Oxbridge degree. One might imagine, then, that he would have been particularly daunted by his weekly audiences with the Queen. Not a bit of it. He was, we're told, utterly respectful but winningly relaxed. The Queen liked him, and the feeling was reciprocated. Major always insisted that the conversations were private and frank, and to reveal any details would "destroy forever the bond of trust that exists" between monarch and prime minister. It is clear, however, that his counsel was sympathetic and helpful, especially when it came to confronting the Queen's deep constitutional concerns about having a separated and, perhaps later, a divorced Prince of Wales.

Private Cabinet files, which became available in 2017, confirm an even more determined pro-Windsor campaign. Ministers were told to adopt "strong expressions of support for the institution of monarchy", efforts were redoubled to change the privacy laws in order to shield the royals from overly intrusive scrutiny, and it was Major's idea to rush through the crowd-pleasing announcement about the Queen's willingness to pay tax on her private income. He had earned his invitations to the occasional informal barbecue at Balmoral.

John Major proved to be a great support, and sounding board, for the Queen during a difficult year

A year in which state visits became almost a respite from the royal family's troubles: the sultan of Brunei is welcomed by the Queen and Prince Philip in November

Prince Andrew looking suitably glum in July 1992

head and the separation was announced on 19 March. The duchess did not simply vanish from the scene and at the start of August she was even to be found at the royal breakfast table at Balmoral. Unfortunately, the morning papers were being passed around and one contained photos of Fergie sunbathing topless and having her toes kissed by her new beau John Bryan. A mortified Sarah Ferguson soon received her marching orders.

Next on the docket were Princess Anne and her husband, Mark Phillips. They had been separated since 1989, hardly ever appeared in public together, and had developed a taste for quarreling about money and their private lives. It came as no great surprise when they divorced on 23 April 1992. A magistrate at Somerset House took just four minutes to enact the decision and neither party was required to attend. Still, a great deal of acrimony lay behind this rubber-stamping and Anne was married to Timothy Laurence before the end of the year.

Such partings ended up being something of a side-show when compared with the unravelling

of the relationship between Prince Charles and Lady Diana. The so-called 'war of the Waleses' had been raging for quite some time, but during 1992 the stakes were raised and an indecorous feud became utterly bizarre.

On 7 June, Andrew Morton's *Diana: Her True Story* hit, and subsequently flew off, the shelves. It was a warts-and-all story, though the royal family appeared to possess all the warts. Charles' alleged affair with Camilla Parker Bowles took centre stage and Diana was portrayed as a woman in dire emotional straits. The bulimia, the self-harm and even a possible suicide attempt were all recounted. To the Queen's great annoyance, it quickly became clear that Diana's friends had happily supplied information to Morton, though Diana's own direct, substantial contribution was not fully revealed until after her death in 1997.

Things became even more unseemly later in the year with the arrival of Squidgygate. The press got hold of a phone conversation (dating from New Year's Eve 1989) in which the princess let off steam to her friend James Gilbey (who had a habit

An already sombre occasion with an extra layer of awkwardness: Princesses Diana and Anne alongside the Queen Mother performing balcony duty on Remembrance Day

THE LIMITS OF SYMPATHY

The British public exhibited a measured kind of sympathy for the Queen during these frantic months. No-one wants to see a family fall apart, but many couldn't help but remark that these, at bottom, were really just unedifying domestic tiffs. As for the Windsor fire, yes, it was a tragedy, but when the nation was informed that it would have to foot the bill for repairs (estimated at £30-40 million and finally coming in at £36.5 million), generosity of spirit began to recede. The castle was not insured so public funds would have to be raided. All at a time of recession and in a country where the Queen paid no tax on her private income. The journalist Janet Daley remarked that "when the castle stands it is theirs... but when it burns down it is ours". As an anonymous courtier put it, the cash demands "really got the national goat".

To her credit, the Queen agreed to do the right thing, She and Prince Charles would now stump up their tax contributions (as many earlier monarchs and heirs to the throne had done), payments to those on the Civil List would be reduced, and the size of the list would shrink: the Queen would now fund those who didn't make the cut. She would also cover 70 per cent of the renovation costs at the castle, even agreeing to open Buckingham Palace to public visitors in order to swell the coffers.

By year's end, during the annual Christmas Day message, a slight shift in language and tone could be detected. The Queen was careful to place her woes in perspective, explaining that "like many other families we have lived through some difficult days". Also, the annus horribilis line was replaced by the less theatrical phrase 'a sombre year'.

Funnily enough, and as a side note, it turns out that 'annus horribilis' wasn't, strictly speaking, perfect Latin. It had originated with the retired courtier Edward Ford who had included it in a letter to the Queen. Ford admitted that he should probably have used annus horrendus to describe a horrid year, because horribilis carries more of a sense of something that is capable of scaring. And scared, the Queen never was. The play on words and contrast with the phrase annus mirabilis was presumably just too hard to resist. The British monarchy had, after all, enjoyed its share of wonderful years, and the phrase is most often applied to 1759, during which the British racked up famous victories against the French in the Seven Years' War and even managed to capture Quebec. As many a royalist must have mused at the end of 1992, those were the days.

A smaller, but faithful version of an important painting destroyed during the Windsor fire: William Beechey's depiction of George III

The Sun newspaper, which, naturally, was ecstatic. The paper ran the Squidgygate transcripts on 24 August 1992. Then some puzzling questions began to be asked. Could Reenan really have just happened upon the call - conducted via two mobile phones, miles apart? Detailed analyses of the tape showed some odd discrepancies and strange noises in the background. Sinister words like bugging, tampering

During the short visit to France in June 1992, the Queen was captured smiling with striking frequency. A master class in putting a brave face on things, or proof that getting away from turmoil at home was the best tonic?

and leaking became part of the debate, as did the idea of some kind of plot. Might this have been a backlash from Charles' supporters: an attempt to portray Diana as unhinged? Might those at the very heart of power - even MI5 - have been involved?

It was a good time for the conspiracy theorists, but also for those who wondered, in a more measured way, if something just wasn't quite right with the whole affair. One certainty is available: this was the death knell of the marriage. Coincidentally, Charles met with Diana on the day following the Queen's Guildhall speech and announced that he would be seeking a formal separation. The prime minister, John Major, broke the news to the House of Commons on 9 December.

referring to Diana as "Squidgy"). Diana had been in the mood for a rant. Charles, she said, "makes my life torture"; the Queen Mother had a curious way of looking at her - a mixture of condescension, pity and fascination. Even Diana's interest in clairvoyance got an airing.

The narrative of where the recording came from was, at first, a little strange but fairly straightforward. An amateur radio enthusiast in Oxfordshire, Cyril Reenan, somehow managed to pick up the conversation on his scanner. He sat on his tapes for a while, then decided to contact

"BY YEAR'S END, DURING THE ANNUAL CHRISTMAS DAY MESSAGE, A SLIGHT SHIFT IN LANGUAGE AND TONE COULD BE DETECTED"

©Getty, Alamy

The arrival of Prince George in 2013 guaranteed the direct line of succession from the Queen would continue for many decades to come

THE MODERN MONARCHY

The 21st century has been filled with record-breaking moments for Elizabeth II, but she has kept her focus on preparing the royal family for the future

A s the Diamond Jubilee celebrations for Elizabeth II reached their climax in the summer of 2012, the monarch appeared on the balcony of Buckingham Palace with tens of thousands of people cheering her from the Mall. The Queen, sparkling in diamond white, took centre stage, but the royals who appeared around her looked very different, for just five other members of her family stood alongside her on that special day. The message was clear: the 21st-century monarchy was all about the Queen and her direct heirs.

The new face of this ancient institution had never been clearer. But what was also on show on 5 June 2012 was the transition Elizabeth II was overseeing from her own record-breaking reign to the rule of her successor. The small group of 'core' royals who greeted the crowds at her jubilee was an idea promoted passionately behind palace walls by the Prince of Wales. Prince Charles was certain that for the monarchy to modernise it had to focus on just a handful of members, stripping back the layers of HRHs who had been on public duty for much of Elizabeth II's reign. This public appearance was the Queen's backing for his plans, and it signalled another subtle shift in the royal rule of Elizabeth II.

The Queen had already spent much of her long reign addressing the increasing challenges of keeping the monarchy relevant in modern society. Her support for a slimmed-down structure was a nod to the future, given while she oversaw a model of royal engagement that had served her for decades. Her cousins, the duke of Gloucester and the duke of Kent, continued to carry out hundreds of duties on her behalf across the UK every year, while her only daughter, the Princess Royal, regularly outstripped every other member of her family as she racked up dozens of engagements a week. But while their steadfast support for the monarchy continued, the Queen, with the support of her heir, began to explore new ways of making the royal family relevant to the country it served.

The ideas had first taken shape in the 1990s when senior royals and their advisers formed the Way Ahead Group. This informal organisation met several times a year to discuss modernisation. By the time the 21st century had dawned, several of its ideas had altered the working lives of the Windsors. Royal engagements were spread more widely across the country, while the guest lists for the Queen's annual garden parties at Buckingham Palace and Holyroodhouse were shaken up to make them more representative of modern society. But the Queen also oversaw a process that moved the focus of royal appearances towards major projects and ongoing schemes.

This change became clear in 2016 when the duke and duchess of Cambridge, along with Prince Harry, launched their Heads Together campaign, which put the spotlight on mental health issues. The project was designed to be ongoing, with new platforms launched on a regular basis and in association with other organisations.

Heads Together came two years after Prince Harry introduced the Invictus Games to the world.

The Queen was deeply concerned Prince Charles should inherit her role as Head of the Commonwealth and made a personal appeal to leaders for their backing

THE MOST HISTORIC DAY OF ALL

The Queen wasn't keen to celebrate when she overtook Queen Victoria

"Inevitably, a long life can pass many milestones - my own is no exception." With that discreet sentence, spoken in Scotland on 9 September 2015, Elizabeth II acknowledged an event that had made headlines around the world. For she was speaking on the day that she became the longest-reigning monarch in British history, and while she was keen to play the moment down, others were more than ready to celebrate.

The bells of Westminster Abbey peeled in celebration of the event while Tower Bridge opened as a fleet of boats, led by the barge Gloriana, processed down the Thames to honour the Queen. Business in the House of Commons was put back by half an hour so that MPs could pay tribute to Elizabeth II with the then-prime minister, David Cameron, describing her record-breaking rule as a "golden thread running through... generations".

The star of the show spent the day opening a new railway in the Scottish Borders. But as she travelled through the countryside by train, Elizabeth II left her seat to stand at a window as she realised crowds of people were spontaneously lining the route to pay tribute to her on this most historic day.

Elizabeth II's success in keeping royalty relevant was clear to see as crowds packed grass verges to see her as she travelled by train on the day she became Britain's longest-reigning monarch

His concept of an international sporting event for injured service personnel caught the public imagination, with the original London event becoming the springboard for regular competitions held around the world. Meanwhile, the duchess of Cambridge oversaw a series of projects focusing on child and maternal wellbeing, and in 2020 launched a nationwide survey designed to inform future structures for early years childcare. The Queen's blessing was evident, with public praise for the initiatives voiced regularly.

As royalty changes in the 21st century, the Queen has supported the younger generation in promoting long-term causes and projects

The younger royals were still expected to carry out more traditional duties too, and as the 2010s progressed, Elizabeth II began the process of handing over some of the 600 patronages she held to the next generation. These honorary roles are seen by the Windsors as a way of lending support to important causes and organisations, and many have been passed from senior royal to senior royal for decades. As the Queen marked her 90th birthday, she announced that several of the most high-profile patronages on her list would be passed on. But while the aim was to reduce her own workload, she was also aware that the interest in the younger members of her family would bring new support to these traditional roles. Just two years later, as the duchess of Cambridge stepped forward to present the trophy at the Men's Final at Wimbledon having inherited the role of patron there from the Queen, that aim became clear. Kate's picture was beamed around the world, boosting one of the UK's biggest sporting events further.

It also gave a further indication of how modernising the monarchy in the 21st century meant planning for a future without the Queen. As the 2010s came to an end, Elizabeth II put all her energies into ensuring that her heir, Prince Charles, would inherit a treasured role that wasn't guaranteed to pass to him on her death. In 2018, she publicly stated that she wanted her eldest son to become head of the Commonwealth once he inherited her crown. Her address to the Commonwealth Heads of Government Meeting in London, attended by many members of her wider royal family to boost her plans, led to the organisation officially declaring Charles would inherit the role carried out by his mother and his grandfather before him.

In recent years, the duke and duchess of Cambridge have taken on a more senior role and often meet with heads of state, such as Indian Prime Minister Narendra Modi

That focus on the Prince of Wales was an increasing part of the Queen's plans for the 21st-century monarchy as her reign progressed. She decided to scale back her overseas travel and in 2015 carried out her last outgoing state visit. At the same time, the Prince of Wales began to increase his foreign travel with an intense programme of official visits to promote Britain in other countries. His itinerary continued to follow the pattern set by the Queen, which had seen her make ground-breaking trips including the first state visit to the Republic of Ireland by a British monarch. In 2019, Prince Charles continued that model as he and the duchess of Cornwall became the first UK royals to tour Cuba. The sight of a future king laying a wreath with the famous image of Che Guevara in the background was a moment of modernisation both Charles and the Queen had worked to achieve.

The king-in-waiting has since taken on a more high-profile role in the affairs of state that remain the core of the Queen's role. The decision by the

The Queen has become used to people trying to get selfies as she walks past

"LIKE HER GRANDFATHER, ELIZABETH II HAS ALWAYS RECOGNISED THE POWER OF THE MEDIA"

duke of Edinburgh to retire from public life in 2017 led to the Prince of Wales accompanying his mother to major national events including the State Opening of Parliament.

As the 2010s came to an end, the sight of Charles on the throne in the House of Lords became a regular event, another public sign of things to come. When the controversial state visit of President Donald Trump took place in London in 2019, it was the prince who accompanied his mother on this very modern outing, watching as the US leader touched down by helicopter in the grounds of Buckingham Palace. It was an indication that even the most ancient of traditions isn't set in stone, and that the transition between Elizabeth and Charles is about moving the monarchy forward.

The Queen learned the importance of keeping up with the public mood from her grandparents. King George V and Queen Mary had both been skilled PR experts, even changing the name of their dynasty to protect it from protesting voices. Like her grandfather, Elizabeth II always recognised the power of the media, and as the 21st century progressed, so didher attitude towards it. The traditional Christmas speech was occasionally been filmed outside of her favourite homes of Windsor Castle and Sandringham, while the Queen and her

family engaged in a series of TV programmes to mark special events, including a rare interview with the monarch herself to mark the 65th anniversary of her coronation.

Social media has also become an important tool in the modern press strategy. The royal family launched its official Twitter account in 2009 with the Prince of Wales adding his own, @ClarenceHouse, a year later. By the time the duke and duchess of Cambridge added @KensingtonRoyal to the social media stable, it had become a major outlet for royal news. Official Facebook and YouTube channels also shared the stories the royals wanted people to know about, while the spike in popularity of Instagram in the late 2010s led to another raft of social media outlets for the Windsors, with the account of the duke and duchess of Sussex breaking records for follower numbers on the day it was launched in 2019.

Managing this new form of interaction brought issues for the Queen's modernisation plans. The decision by Harry and Meghan to step back from their roles as senior royals was published on Instagram in January 2020, just minutes after the couple informed their relatives that they were going to make the announcement. Traditional media outlets soon reported disappointment within the

CREATING THE IMAGE OF A 21ST-CENTURY QUEEN

The style of a modern monarch has largely been shaped by one woman

While the younger members of her family, including the duchess of Cambridge, have become style icons in the 21st century, the Queen has revitalised her own image under the guidance of her trusted dresser, Angela Kelly.

Born in Liverpool, Kelly became personal assistant to the Queen in 2002. The majority of the monarch's outfits since then were the work of the woman who also holds the title of Senior Dresser. In fact, Kelly became so trusted that the Queen even took the rare step of giving her blessing to a book she published in 2019. In it, she revealed they were so close that she even wore in the Queen's new shoes for her so that they were comfortable enough to use during long public engagements.

Throughout the 21st century, Kelly oversaw a restyling of the monarch's wardrobe, subtly modernising her trusted combination of dresses and coats to produce a more up-to-date take on Elizabeth II's classic look. One thing, though, remained the same: the Queen was always seen with her famous black handbag, which was carried over one arm for decades.

Kelly's designs featured in a 2016 exhibition at Buckingham Palace dedicated to the Queen's evolving style

©Getty

royal family at the timing of the move, and weeks of intense scrutiny followed before the Queen issued a statement outlining how the future roles of the duke and duchess would develop.

But even that announcement was very different from the press interaction in earlier parts of Elizabeth II's reign. The personal nature of the statement, as she called her grandson and his wife by their first names, and her focus on their wellbeing, highlighted another change. The royal family had faced criticism in the past for appearing cold and uncaring, even towards each other. The royal reaction to the tragic death of Princess Diana

percentage of the profits generated by the Crown Estate used to fund the work of the royal family. The rise of the internet means accounts and detailed breakdowns of how that cash is spent are available online every year, adding a new element of transparency to royal revenues.

However, royal finances remain a touchy subject. Criticism in 2016 over the use of public funds to renovate Buckingham Palace was the latest in a string of financial issues that have also raised questions over younger members of the royal family using their connections to make money. The Queen's eldest grandson, Peter Phillips, came

early part of the 21st century, didn't receive the royal styles that they were entitled to use and are instead known as Lady Louise Windsor and Viscount Severn. Most of her great-grandchildren have no royal title, while the Queen has also been far more lenient than her predecessors when it comes to picking baby names. Her approval is generally sought by new parents for their choices, but the 21st century has seen the traditional range including Victoria and Albert replaced by modern selections like Archie and Savannah.

It's a small concession but a vital one to keep the monarchy relevant. It was also another indication of the Queen's continuing efforts to move with the times. Aware that remarriage is increasingly common, she openly supported two of her divorced children and steered all her descendants away from the pressures of arranged matches.

"THE SUSSEXES' DECISION ALSO THRUST THE SPOTLIGHT ON HOW THE ROYAL FAMILY IS FUNDED"

in 1997 was particularly unpopular with the British public. When dealing with Harry and Meghan's departure, the Queen was determined that a more modern, gentle approach should be followed.

The Sussexes' decision also thrust the spotlight once more on how the royal family is funded. The Queen had already tried to bring her family's finances forward with her decision to pay tax. In 2012 the Civil List, the annual grant from Parliament that covers some of the expenses of the monarch and their family, was replaced with the Sovereign Grant. The new arrangement sees a

under fire for advertising milk in China, and there was widespread debate about whether Harry and Meghan would use their royal brand to achieve the financial independence they announced they were seeking as they decided to change direction.

The Queen showed an acute awareness of the issues facing those born into her family, but with no clear future role in the Firm's development. She was keen to use titles, or the lack thereof, to underline the distinction between the public and private sides of being part of the Windsors. Her youngest son's two children, born in the

The focus of the monarchy remained the Queen until her last, and her historic reign continued to keep her at the heart of royal life. Celebrations for major milestones, including breaking the record for longest-ruling British monarch in 2015, saw an outpouring of public support for Elizabeth II even when other members of her family faced criticism. However, her reaction to these landmarks, always muted and measured, was designed to ensure that her own star power didn't become so central to the royal family that it failed as soon as it was removed.

The image of the Queen on the balcony at her Diamond Jubilee, at the heart of a slimmed-down monarchy, only underlined the work that Elizabeth II put into developing her family so that it was more than ready to face the future.

The Queen and Prince Philip attend the Braemar Gathering, something that brought both of them much joy